Law and Practice for Security Professionals

Damien Buckland

Edition published 2013 by Damien Buckland

ISBN-13: 978-1493723539

ISBN-10: 1493723537

©2013 Damien Buckland

All rights reserved. No part of this book may be reprinted or reproduced or utilised in any form or by any electronic, mechanical, or other means, now known or hereafter invented, including photocopying and recording, or in any information storage or retrieval system, without permission in writing from the publisher.

All photographs used are with the express permission of the copyright owner or are free of restrictions for use in commercial purposes where applicable.

CONTENTS

The Law and the Charge (a difference)?	13
The English Legal System	15
Types of crime (Conduct or Result)	17
Civil and Criminal Proceedings	19
Criminal liability of juveniles	20
Ignorance of the law	22
Summary, indictable, & either-way offences	22
Requirements for a criminal wrongdoing	24
An offence in failing to act	26
Special relationships	26
Contractual duty to act	26
Statutory duty to act	27
The defendant who creates a dangerous situation	27
Accomplice liability	28
The Theft Act 1968	33
Theft	34
Theft by consumption	40
Ticket-swapping	41
Using a child to commit the theft	42

Stealing your own property	43
Obtaining property by mistake	43
Robbery	47
Burglary	52
Aggravated burglary	61
Removal of articles from places open to the public	64
Taking a motor vehicle or other conveyance without authority	67
Aggravated vehicle taking	70
Abstracting of electricity	73
Joyriding in a lift	74
Handling stolen goods	75
Advertising reward for goods lost or stolen	79
Going equipped for stealing	81
Making off without payment	83
Fraud Act 2006	87
Fraud by false representation	88
Fraud by failing to disclose information	91
Fraud by abuse of position	92
Possession of articles for use in fraud	93
Obtaining services dishonestly	93

The Guard Dogs Act 1975	96
The Court Security Officer (Designation) Regulation 2005	101
Powers of arrest	103
The Criminal Damage Act 1971	107
Destroying or damaging property	107
Aggravated criminal damage (agg. Arson)	111
Arson	
Threats to destroy or damage Property	113
Possessing anything with intent to destroy or damage property	114
Assaults	115
Common assault	115
Battery	118
The Offences Against the Person Act 1861	118
Assault occasioning actual bodily Harm	119
Wounding or inflicting grievous bodily harm	121
Wounding or inflicting grievous	

bodily harm with intent	122
Unintentional contact	124
The Use of force	126
The Criminal Attempts Act 1981	129
Human Rights in brief	134
The Private Security Industry Act 2001	137
The SIA	137
Licensing	138
Vehicle immobilisation	139
SIA Licences	139
In-house guarding	140
Approved contractor scheme	140
Data Protection Act 1998	141
Rights afforded to the citizen	141
Data protection principles & their relation to CCTV	142
Trespass	146
Neighbours boundaries	147
Deterring trespassers	147
Table of cases	149
Table of legislation	150

What ties us all together? Our necessity to abide by and to apply the law!!

The UK security industry is rapidly growing and will continue to increase both in size and complexity over the coming years.

A Security Professional is now a career choice, to develop and progress through, rather than just a job to pay the bills. Combine this with ever increasing legislative procedures, increased crime rate, and far more complex tasks and you find that a career in the security industry today offers far more variety and practice than many other areas of employment.

Going back over the past fifty years, the roll of a Security Officer would usually involve standing on a building site on a cold winter's night ensuring that youngsters didn't climb the fence and pinch anything. An Officer may deal with this by marching the aforementioned youngster to their parent's house to be dealt with appropriately. An Officer working in a specialist area would usually be highly qualified and would rarely rise from the ranks. Store Detectives were only ever used in very large, very well established, stores. Loss Prevention defined the role of a company Manager or Director, and usually one with no idea of losses through illegal activity. Door Supervisors were usually locals from the bar offered a few free drinks to throw out the trouble and Close Protection was carried out only by Police and Military.

Today things have changed dramatically and so has the complexity of the legal processes we must each adhere to. There is a fine line between upholding the law and breaking the law. In modern days you are expected to prevent crime, protect life and property, and help bring to justice those who break the law, as well as ensure a continuality of evidence, maintain safety standards and yet still serve the needs and requirements of your employer and contractor.

This is not a book designed to teach you to 'suck eggs'. We will not paraphrase the law and expect you to understand and remember it. You will not be taught the basic definitions of crimes of which you will probably already have a clear idea about. What you will do is learn to break down various offences which, as a Security Professional you will come across on a daily basis. Once these offences are broken down you will understand the evidential requirements of each offence and how the Prosecution Services will look at both the offence committed and your work dealing with it.

What I mean by this is that I think I can safely assume that you have an appropriate understanding of offences such as Theft or Burglary, but do you know how to break down the Theft Act of 1968? What about the same Act, but of 1978? Do you understand the legal and evidential requirements of a particular crime you have observed? What section would an act of theft occur if the item was eaten rather than concealed and would we still have a theft? At what stage of the 'theft' has the appropriate offence been committed? You will probably think it is when the person has exited the store? Right?? Wrong! What if the thief already owns the property?? Puzzled yet??

Do you understand when the offence of Burglary has been committed? When the offender trespasses and commits a theft?? Ok... What if the offender does not enter the building but instead only puts one arm inside the building and punches the victim in the head? Still Burglary??

Clear understandings of these offences and the legislation that surrounds them is of paramount importance to every Officer working within the United Kingdom.

Legislation will be clearly laid out and explained in simple to understand language, giving examples to help you understand them. Many offences are accompanied by their appropriate Criminal Prosecution guidelines. These allow you to understand what the prosecution services and the Courts will be looking for when dealing with any offence you have dealt with. It will mean that you can gear you statement to include this information and increase the chances of successful prosecutions.

Warning!!! Time spent with this book will result in a far greater understanding of some areas of the law than the Police you work alongside. You will understand not only the law surrounding your work but how to use those laws to your advantage. How to 'play' with the system instead of working as its minion. There is no need to have a higher than average brain function. Much of what you will learn is taught as part of the same Law Degree which Solicitors and Barristers have. Only now you will also have the same knowledge and understanding. You will know how not to let the offenders get away with it because their solicitor has twisted an area of your statement to make their client appear a saint rather than a crook and you will understand where the boundaries are between you upholding the law, and breaking the law.

We will therefore learn:

- To guide each Officer on correct practice and procedure and to remain within all legal remits.
- To further advance your knowledge of legal bargaining tools and the strategies that are available to you.
- To enhance your knowledge of legal procedures and evidential burdens.
- We all know when a person has done something wrong... but do we always know when it is legally wrong?
- To learn how the law works, what each offence really means and how to classify the offence committed.

THE LAW AND THE CHARGE (A DIFFERENCE)?

Through this book you will learn to clearly define and break down each criminal offence and understand the requirements of law. But let's say, for example, you gain this knowledge and are able to break down an act of theft into its core components to determine that an act you have witnessed is in fact a burglary or false representation? Would you arrest or you're your complaint under these offences??

Quite simply "no". Any arrest or prosecution should be based upon the Act you are working under, so an apprehension for burglary would lead you to arrest or complain of 'Theft' because burglary is an offence under the Theft Act 1968. False representation would lead to an arrest or complaint of 'Fraud' because the offence of fraud by false representation comes under the Fraud Act 2006. The Police and Criminal Prosecution Services will later determine which section of the Theft Act they will prosecute under. 9 times out of 10 the Criminal Prosecution Services will take the simplest option and prosecute for Theft as this is easier to prove and guarantees a much better chance of a conviction.

Now, you may say, "what is the point in me determining an act of burglary or false representation when it may never be used as?" Well… If you are aware that the offence created is in fact a more specific section of the Theft Act 1968 or Fraud Act 2006 then you are now able to gear your statements and evidential collection to that of the specific offence.

Likewise, many offences you will later read about would not be worthy of any prosecution and would instead require your discretion to deal with. A good example of this would be 'joyriding in a lift', which you will learn about later and comes under the offence of 'Abstracting Electricity' (Section 13 of the Theft Act 1968). You would quite simply never arrest, or detain for this, as the losses to your employer are so insignificant that it would be a waste of everybody's time to take it further.

You will however have the knowledge and understanding to determine that an offence has/is being committed and that you are able to deal with this appropriately.

THE ENGLISH LEGAL SYSTEM

Firstly, for the sake of interest only, let us take a quick look at where the English Legal system actually came from...

English law comes from a 'Common law' legal system. This means that our laws started off, not with some medieval form of Parliament but, with the decisions of judges after it was felt a person had committed a wrong and needed to be punished.

So the first person to be convicted of a certain crime, let us take for example 'murder', would most probably have been some man in a village somewhere in England or Wales who beat another to death and was then hauled before the local justices by an angry mob of towns folk all yearning for retribution. The local justices (or judges as we would know them) would have decided that what the man had done was wrong (not forgetting that as yet there are no written laws to determine the wrong). The judge would have then sentenced the perpetrator to whatever form of punishment he felt the killer deserved and declared that to murder another person is wrong. This effectively became law and set a precedent for all future 'trials' of the same crime and is known as stare decisis'. So when somebody 'murdered' another person in the next village over, the judge could say "that is against the law and we know this because it has already been decided in that other village across the way". Now, several hundred years later, when one person intentionally kills another it is still murder and is still a common (or judge-made) law. There is no written piece of legislation saying that it is an offence to murder someone. The courts know it is illegal because that judge in that village in medieval times decided it so.

Laws made nowadays (and for the past 300 years) are made by Parliament and are known as 'Acts of Parliament' or 'legislation'. As a result, the English and Welsh legal system is now made up of 'judge-made' law, written legislation and, since the 1st of January 1973, European Law. Legislation is supreme and so where there is a confliction between the laws made by judges of old and Parliamentary legislation, the legislation will win hands down and the judge made law disregarded. Where legislation conflicts with European law, legislation is still supreme but the courts are instructed to interpret laws in accordance with European law.

CONDUCT & RESULT CRIMES

Crimes are defined as either 'conduct' or 'result' crimes. The difference is simple enough:

Conduct crimes occur when the offenders behaviour is prohibited (for example being drunk and disorderly or attempting to blackmail another person). This means that the offender has committed an offence the moment they behave that way no matter what the outcome. So if the offender tries to blackmail another person they have committed an offence regardless of whether they actually accomplish it successfully.

Result crimes mean that the offence does not apply until the act has been completed. An example of this would be 'murder'. There can be no offence of murder until the act has been completed and the victim is dead and so the 'result' applies. If the offender fails to kill then he or she could have committed an 'attempted murder' which would be a conduct crime again because the offence is being committed as they are proceeding with it.

Conduct Crimes = the behaviour is the offence prohibited by law.

Result Crimes = the end result of that behaviour is the offence prohibited by law.

CIVIL AND CRIMINAL PROCEEDINGS

The English legal system consists of both civil and criminal proceedings.

Civil proceedings are held in civil courts (such as a County Court) and are usually started by the person who has suffered a loss so the court will usually impose some type of financial redress to compensate the victim. The victim can accept compensation outside of the courts (known as a 'settlement' and most civil proceedings will result in this). The victim is able to discontinue proceedings at any stage should they decide not to pursue the case any further. The ultimate aim of civil proceedings is to compensate the victim.

Criminal proceedings are held in criminal courts (such as a Magistrate's Court or Crown Court) and are usually brought by the criminal prosecution services, even if the victim does not wish to complain (and in some rare occasions private prosecutions can be brought by the victim if the prosecution services do not wish to proceed). They will usually impose some form of punishment to the offender should they be found guilty. In some cases the victim can except compensation ordered by the courts, and to be paid by the offender, although the primary aim of criminal proceedings is to punish the offender rather than compensate the victim.

Civil proceedings = County Court and held by a Judge with the aim of correcting a 'wrong' or compensating the 'victim'.

Criminal proceedings = Magistrates' Court before a Magistrate or Crown Court before a Judge and Jury with the aim of punishing the offender for a criminal wrong.

CIVIL RECOVERY

Most Officers' working within the retail security sector will have at some point come across Civil Recovery law firms. These companies will compensate the shop or other business for any wrongs caused to them by the actions of, for example, a shoplifter. They do this by taking the 'wrongdoer' to a civil court and having the Court order them to pay a certain amount in financial reparation. This does not mean that the wrongdoer is hauled before the Judge and told to pay huge amounts of money because they have been very, very, bad.

The Civil Recovery law firm (Claimant) will approach the Civil Courts and request compensation to be paid to them on behalf of 'Whatever' store. The compensation will cover any losses incurred by the store as a result of the wrongful actions of the 'shoplifter'. These losses will include everything from the cost of unsaleable goods, any equipment damaged, the cost of CCTV tapes and discs. In fact pretty much everything they can claim for, they will. The law firm making the claim does not have to 'prove' the offender is guilty of these losses. They only have to show on a 'balance of probabilities' that the offender is responsible for these losses. So if the Claimant (Civil Recovery firm) claims that the offender committed 'such and such' wrong on 'such and such' date and this incurred 'such and such' losses, then, on a balance of probabilities, they are probably right. If the offender disputes this then they can argue the order, but generally they do not.

CRIMINAL LIABILITY OF JUVENILES

Most countries have a minimum age whereby a person can be found to have committed a criminal offence. This is simply because a young child may not know, or be expected to know, that something they have done is criminally wrong.

In England and Wales the age at which a child is criminally liable is 10 years old. This means that any child under the age of 10 is considered by the courts to not know the difference between right or wrong and that they are unable to comprehend that what they have done is wrong or illegal.

England and Wales used to have the defence of 'doli incapax' which meant that although a child could be prosecuted for a criminal offence from the age of 10, if they were between the ages of 10-14 the prosecution would have to prove that the child knew that what he or she had done was 'seriously wrong' and had what could be described as 'mischievous discretion' to be liable for the offence. This defence no longer applies since the Crime and Disorder Act 1998 and a 2009 case in the House of Lords (House of Lords case R v. T [2009] LAC 310) abolished the presumption of doli incapax and so we now have the lowest criminal liability age of anywhere else in Europe.

The law in Scotland is different whereby the legal age of criminal responsibility is 12. Some other countries are higher still, such as Germany (14), Denmark (15) and Belgium (18).

At this time (2013) there are current proposals to increase the age of criminal responsibility from 10 to 12 years. Whether this will happen we shall have to wait and see.

IGNORANCE OF THE LAW

We have all heard the saying "ignorance is no defence to the law". Is it true?

'Yes'. No matter what the circumstances... whether a person is visiting from another country with different laws, is unable to read, has no way of knowing the law or was even advised in error by a police officer or public official, there is no excuse for not knowing it was illegal. "I didn't know" is no excuse.

SUMMARY, INDICTABLE AND EITHER-WAY OFFENCES

When a person is prosecuted for a criminal offence they will attend either a Magistrate's court or a Crown court. The type and/or seriousness of the offence will determine which court they go before.

A Magistrates' court tends to deal with the more minor offences (which are summary offences) and are heard before a Magistrate (also known as a 'JP' or 'Justice of the Peace'). As punishment they can place orders and restrictions or curfews upon the offender, such as electronic tagging or requirement to perform unpaid work up to 300 hours. They can also place supervision orders on an offender up to 3 years. Magistrates can also impose imprisonment up to 6 months for a single offence or 12 months for consecutive offences. Whether an offence is summary is determined by the seriousness of the offence and the written legislation will always state whether the offence is Summary, Indictable or triable either way. Examples of summary offences would be some road traffic offences where the maximum punishment for the particular offence is below 6 months imprisonment.

A Crown Court deals with more serious offences (Indictable offences). These are offences whereby the maximum sentence imposed is higher than the 6 months that can be imposed by a magistrate. An example would be murder or rape where the required punishment will, hopefully, be a bit more than 6 months or a community order. Offenders (or those accused of offences) in the Crown court are seen by Judges. There are three types of judges in a Crown court. They are 'High Court Judges', who tend to deal with the more serious and controversial offences such as murder, and 'Circuit Judges' and 'Recorders'. Circuit Judges and Recorders deal with all other offences in the Crown Court. The Crown Court also uses jury's. The Judge will 'hear' the case and impose the punishment (should the person be found guilty). The jury will hear the trial and decide upon whether they believe the accused by choosing them guilty or not guilty. Where an accused person has plead guilty to the offence then a jury will not be used and the Judge will simply hear the case and decide the appropriate punishment.

Triable either way offences are those offences of which the seriousness of depends on the act performed and can be either summary or indictable offences (hence 'triable either way'). An example of a triable either way offence is 'theft'. Theft can be a minor offence to go before the Magistrate's court or more serious offence whereby a heavier punishment may be required and so go before a Crown Court. So a case of shoplifting where £100 worth of goods was stolen will more than likely go before a Magistrate. A theft involving £50,000 will probably go before a judge in the Crown Court. In some circumstances a Magistrate may decide that the accused person in their court deserves a higher punishment than they can impose for the offence and so will send them for trial to the Crown Court.

REQUIREMENTS FOR A CRIMINAL WRONGDOING

For a person to have committed a criminal 'wrong' they must have achieved three separate requirements:

1.   'Actus reus' - The offender must have committed a 'guilty act'. This means they must have physically done what they are accused of.

2.   'Mens rea' - The offender must have had a guilty mind (or have been reckless). This means that the offender must have intended to commit the offence (or have been reckless as to having committed it). An exception to this would be in rare 'strict liability' offences where a guilty mind is not

required, only that the person has done the act. As a general rule within the private security industry you will rarely come upon strict liability offences (if ever) and so will be looking for the guilty mind.

3. 'An absence of any valid defence' – As it says… If there is a valid defence (one specifically accepted by law and not just an 'excuse') then there can be no offence.

So let us put these requirements towards an act of theft. A person takes property belonging to another (you will go deeper into this later as we progress through the Theft Act 1968). When the offender physically takes the property then they have committed the 'actus reus' of theft. If they intended to do so and had within their mind the intention to commit theft then we have the 'mens rea'. If the person does not have any valid defence (for example they were not entitled to the property by law or did not have a court order enabling them to remove the property) then they have an absence of any valid defence. If the accused person has now fulfilled all of these requirements then we have an offence of theft.

AN OFFENCE IN FAILING TO ACT

Most criminal charges involve the offender having done something illegal (such as stealing a car, burning a house down, murdering a person, etc...). But what about offences of failing to do something? Can a person be prosecuted for not doing an act?

In the majority of cases 'no'. But there are four key principles where a failure to act can result in criminal liability:

1)   Special relationships

Where there is a 'special relationship' between the offender and the victim either because the offender has a particular duty owed to the victim or because of family ties. For example, a parent has a duty to care for their young child. If they fail to do this appropriately (for example not feeding him or her) then that failure to act could be a criminal offence under section 1(2) of the Children and Young Persons Act (1933) by "neglecting him in a manner likely to cause injury to his health if he has failed to provide adequate food, clothing, medical aid or lodging for him".

2)   A contractual duty to act

A person can be liable for failing to act where they have a contractual duty to do something. This does not necessarily mean somebody signs a piece of paper agreeing to do something and then failing to do it. If a carer is responsible as part of his or her job to give a patient lifesaving medication and then fails to do this, resulting in the patient's death, then the carer is criminally liable. Not for failing to give medication but for failing to act as they were contractually obliged to.

A contractual duty to act comes from case law (R v. Pittwood (1902) 19 TLR 37) whereby a railway crossing keeper failed to activate his crossing in time, resulting in a train crashing and a number of deaths. The railway crossing keeper was held liable for the deaths because he failed to perform his contractual duty.

3) Statutory duty to act

Where there is a legal requirement to do something and a person fails to do it. Examples of this are where a person fails to display a valid tax disc on their car or fails to stop at a red traffic light.

4) The defendant who creates a dangerous situation

When a person, or persons, create a dangerous situation and then, after realising their error, they fail to take steps to prevent it. So for example, a gas engineer leaves the gas turned on in someone's house and then, realising his or her mistake, fails to make an effort to return to switch it off, evacuate the house, call emergency services, etc… If the house blows up and kills its occupants then the gas engineer is liable for the deaths.

ACCOMPLICE LIABILITY

Either way or Indictable offence.

Maximum penalty = dependent upon the maximum penalty of the principle parties offence (so if the principle offence was theft (up to ten years imprisonment), then the accomplice liability would also be a maximum of ten years, if the principle offence was murder (life imprisonment), then the accomplice liability is also life imprisonment.

When a person commits a crime, they are known as the 'principle offender' (or 'co-principle' offenders where there are more than one). A person who merely 'assists' in the crime is an 'accomplice'.

Accomplice liability is laid out under section 8 of the Accessories and Abettors Act 1861,

"whosoever shall aid, abet, counsel or procure the commission of an offence shall be tried... and punished as a principle offender".

This, quite simply, means that if the 'accomplice' only assisted in the commission of the offence they shall be prosecuted and punished in the same way as the main offender/offenders regardless of whether they were involved in the carrying out of that offence or were actually there at the time.

Aid

Means to "give help, support or assistance to" and usually, but not always, involves the accomplice being present at the crime (such as the 'lookout' person or 'get-away driver').

Abet

Means "to incite, instigate or encourage". The accomplice would always be at the scene of the crime and does not necessarily have to expressly encourage the offence; they could also make an implied agreement about the commission of the offence. So a person will abet an offence whether they say "go and steal that diamond watch and we will go halves on the profit" as well as if they say "if you go and steal that watch we could go halves on the profit". Either way they have still incited instigated or encouraged the offence.

Counsel

Means "to encourage" and would cover where a person gives advice, information or encouragement of the offence. To counsel would also cover where a person supplies the equipment required for the commission of the offence (so where the accomplice supplies the gun for the bank robbers use or gives the lock picks to the burglar, they have 'counselled' the offence).

Procure

Means "to produce by endeavour (effort or attempt), by setting out to see that it happens and taking the appropriate steps to produce that happening". So if a person 'spikes' another person's orange juice in the pub and that person then drives their car (unaware that they have consumed alcohol) and commits a drink-driving offence then the accomplice has procured the offence. The principle offender does not necessarily have to be guilty of the offence. The principle offender in this example would have a defence against drink-driving and so would not be guilty of the offence. The accomplice, on the other hand, would be guilty of a drink-driving offence as they have taken steps to produce that happening. To procure the offence, the accomplice needs to have caused the offence to be committed. So if the driver of the car unknowingly drank the alcohol in his drink but then also knowingly bought himself eight large vodkas, which would have put him over the drink-drive limit, then the accomplice may not be guilty of the offence because it would be hard to prove that the eight large vodkas did not put the driver over the limit but the spiked drink did.

A meeting of the minds?

It is also worth noting that the principle offender does not necessarily have to have even met the accomplice for them to both be guilty of the offence.

For example, the principle offender steals from a

shop... Security Officer Bob is running after the offender to arrest him when John, who is walking down the street, deliberately trips S.O Bob up, thus preventing him from arresting the offender and allowing the offender to get away. John has now assisted the shop lifter in the commission of theft even though they have never met. John is now an accomplice as he has aided the shoplifter and so John could also be charged with the crime of theft.

The accomplice did not think it would happen

It is no defence for the accomplice to claim that they did not believe the principle offender would actually commit the offence. If the accomplice foresees that there is a possibility that the offence will be committed then they will still be an accessory to the actual offence.

In summary

To be clear, let us take for example a shop theft. Three persons are involved in the offence... Mr A, Mr B & Mr C.

Now, Mr A knows of the shop and that the items to remove are on the second aisle on the left in a red box. He tells Mr B and Mr C where these goods are so that they can steal them which they then do. All three are thankfully caught.

Mr B and Mr C have both committed the offence of theft and so are 'co-principles'. Mr A assisted in the commission of the offence by supplying them with the relevant information and so has 'counselled' the offence. All three persons would be charged with the offence of Theft under the Theft Act 1968 and all three offenders are liable to the same punishment of a maximum seven years.

THE THEFT ACT (1968)

Offences under the Theft Act of 1968 are probably the more common offences that a Security Officer will come across in his or her line of work. The Theft Act encompasses a number of different offences against property, from basic theft through to burglary, abstracting electricity, robbery, and more. The offences can be summary or indictable and the maximum sentence given under the Theft Act is life imprisonment.

THEFT

Triable either-way or Indictable offence.

Maximum sentence = 7 years.

Section 1(1) of the Theft Act (1968) determines theft as to:

"dishonestly appropriate property belonging to another with the intention of permanently depriving the owner of it".

Sounds simple doesn't it? But to determine and prove an act of theft we need to break this down into sections...

1. Dishonestly
2. Appropriates
3. Property
4. Belonging to another
5. Intention to permanently deprive

Now, each of the requirements of these five sections needs to be fulfilled to prove an act of theft. If any of these are missing, there is no theft no matter how immoral the perpetrators intention or actions.

Dishonestly

Is the perpetrators act dishonest? Hard to define that isn't it? How do we know that a person had dishonest thoughts?

Section 2 (a)(b)(c) of the Theft Act (1968) describes what is **not** dishonesty with regards to theft:

- if the person takes the property believing, in law, that he has a right to remove it for him/herself or on behalf of another person. *So, for example, if a person removes an item from a shop and does not pay for it they are not guilty of theft if they **genuinely** believed the item did not require payment because it was free or already belonged to them in the first place, etc...*

- if the person takes the property and they

genuinely believed the owner would give their consent. *So, for example, a person removes an item from a shop believing the store owner/manager would let them have it for free then they have not been dishonest and have not committed theft.*

• if a person takes property which they believe belongs to another but they are in the belief that the owner cannot be discovered by taking reasonable steps. *So, as an example, if a person finds property which may have been lost and which they think cannot be returned to its owner by taking reasonable steps then it is not theft. But what are reasonable steps? That is to be decided by the person finding the property and ultimately the courts. It could be argued that if it is in a store then it could have been handed into the store staff or lost property. Perhaps the item was found in the street and so a reasonable step would be to hand it into the Police. Reasonable steps when finding a mobile phone may be to call a number in the phones memory to trace the owner.*

As you can see the definition of dishonesty comes from what is considered not dishonest. If none of these three *excuses* are genuinely available then the action is dishonest and the first stage of theft is applicable.

If the offender claims to have not been dishonest in their actions then the courts can use a method known as 'the Ghosh test' (taken from the criminal case '*R v Ghosh* [1982] EWCA Crim 2', hence it is referred to as the Ghosh test). This involves the jury asking themselves:

1. was the act dishonest according to the ordinary standards of a reasonable and honest person, and
2. would the defendant have realised that reasonable and honest people would regard what he or she did as dishonest? If the jury answer yes to both of these questions then dishonesty is established.

Appropriates

Appropriation means to 'assume the rights of the owner' and is defined by section 3 of the Theft Act 1968. Appropriation does not necessarily only involve taking property to keep. It can also be an appropriation of property if the person uses or interferes with the property in a way which only the owner has a right to do. Those of you who work in retail security may have come across this where a person deliberately swaps the price labels on an item in order to pay a cheaper price. By swapping the price labels they are not taking the item to keep (yet), however, only the store has the right to change the prices labels and anybody else doing so is assuming the rights of the owner and in doing so is appropriating the property irrespective of whether they get away with it or not.

Property

Property has a very broad definition under section

4(1) of the Theft Act (1968). Property can include money or any other item of tangible property (something you can detect by touch). Property can also include 'things in action' which are intangible items (things that you cannot detect with your senses and have no physical being but are accepted as owned by somebody in law). 'Things in action' can include credit card numbers because there is nothing physical in the numbers to literally pick up and take but those unique sets of numbers are owned by a bank somewhere.

A person cannot commit theft of property where the property has been passed to them by a legal order. For example, where they have power of attorney making them the legal representative of the owner where the property is concerned, or a repossession order names that person as having the right to remove it.

Section 4(3) of the Theft Act (1968) states that a person who picks fruit or mushrooms, plants or flowers which are growing wild on land does not commit theft whether the land is privately owned or not. The exception to this would be if they are picking the fruit/mushrooms/plants/flowers to sell on or use for any other commercial purpose. In this case there would be an act of theft.

Wild creatures are considered property under the Theft Act (1968), however unless they are tamed or kept in captivity they cannot be stolen. An example of this would be where wild pigeons are on private land they cannot be stolen because, although they are property, they are not tamed or kept in captivity even if they live on private land. But, if they were racing pigeons, kept in captivity and tamed by their owner then removing these would be theft.

Belonging to another

Property does not necessarily have to belong to the person that bought it. For the purposes of the Theft Act (1968), section 5, makes the property belonging to another as that person in 'possession and control' of it at the time of the theft. This means that if your friend lent you a pen and I stole it from you, although you are not technically the owner, I have still committed the act of theft against you as you are in possession and control of the pen at the time. This covers many scenarios as often a business will have items on their property which are leased or loaned.

If the property has no owner or trustee then it cannot be stolen. This only applies where the property has been completely relinquished by the owner so if a person dumps an item then they would have relinquished all ownership of it and would not expect to ever own that same piece of property again. Therefore to take it would not be theft.

Intention to permanently deprive

A contradiction if any… When a person commits an act of theft it will quite often involve that person intending on not returning the item and so we have an intention to permanently deprive.

However, it gets more complicated than that:

Section 6 of the Theft Act (1968) regards an intention to permanently deprive is even if that person has no intention to cause the owner to permanently lose the property and if the property is to be returned in such a state that all its 'goodness and virtue' is gone. For example, a person takes some batteries without the owner's consent, and then uses the batteries power before returning them. The batteries have still been returned and the owner has not been permanently deprived of them but they have not been returned in the same state. All 'goodness and virtue' has been removed from them. This would still amount to a permanent deprivation under section 6.

To permanently deprive would also include where a person takes an item without the owner's consent but believes they are able to return it in the same state. For example, a person takes property and pawns it with the intention to buy it back later and return it to the original owner. This would still amount to permanently depriving irrespective of whether they would have returned it or not.

COMMON METHODS OF THEFT:

Theft by consumption

This is a generic term as there is no actual offence of theft by consumption; only theft. The consumption is the method used to commit the theft. A person eating property, usually food, without making payment and without the permission of the owner.

When the person puts that item into their mouth then it can no longer be returned in its original state. This means that ownership and control of the property has now been passed to that person and appropriation has now been completed. It will, of course, be permanently deprived as it cannot be given back as it was. The act of theft is completed the moment it enters the person's mouth and that ownership and control has passed over.

Ticket-swapping

As we discussed briefly earlier, a person who changes the price on a product, in order to pay a lower price for the goods, in a shop is doing something with the property that only the owner (the shop) has a right to do. By treating the item as their own (and assuming it is done so dishonestly) they are appropriating the property. It would not be necessary to wait for the offender to purchase the goods at the lower price or wait for them to leave the store as the act of theft has been completed the moment they 'swap' the price ticket. (It should be noted that it is generally good practice to wait for the purchase to take place or the offender to leave the store however to ensure a continuity of evidence and make your case 'watertight'.

Using a child to commit the theft

Another method used by shoplifters regularly is to use a child under the age of criminal responsibility to commit the theft. For example, an adult passes a product to their child under 10 and gets the child to carry the goods out of the store. The idea being that if they are caught then they can blame the child knowing that the child cannot be prosecuted. This is quite a sickening practice to observe, especially knowing that the adult is using their own children to commit the theft. It is however an increasing method being adopted.

So can we still arrest or make a complaint of theft? Yes, of course. The adult is still dishonestly (1) appropriating (2) property (3) which belongs to another (4) with the intention to permanently deprive (5). The only difference is that they are not physically taking the item out of the store themselves but they are using a child to do so. The child, however, is simply a tool or instrument used to conceal and carry the property, just the same as if it were concealed and carried in a bag or back of a pram. The act of theft is still being committed by the adult and so arrest or complaint of theft towards the adult is still perfectly acceptable. The only negative aspect towards this practice is that in some cases dishonesty on behalf of the adult can sometimes be difficult to prove. If the adult claims they knew nothing about the child having possession of the property it can be hard to prove otherwise. This is where good CCTV and/or observation skills and statement writing will play a big part. If you make a good job of this then later prosecution is made all the more likely.

Stealing your own property

Yes you can steal your own property. If I loaned my pen to you then I would have parted with possession and control of it. The possession and control of that pen would become yours and section 5(1) of the Theft Act (1968) regards the 'owner' of the property as that person in possession and control of it. This means that ownership of the pen would now become yours (albeit on a temporary basis). If I then <u>dishonestly</u> took the pen back without your permission then I would be committing the act of theft.

Obtaining property by mistake

The Theft Act (1968) creates a legal obligation for a person to make restoration of the money or property obtained by another person's mistake. So if a person purchases goods at a till point and is given too much change then they have obtained that extra money by another person's (the cashier's) mistake. If the person obtaining the extra money realises the mistake and, through dishonesty, they fail to return it then they have committed theft.

CPS Guidelines on prosecution for theft

Aggravating Factors taken into account when sentencing:

- The theft was part of organised crime
- The offence had professional hallmarks
- Involved a degree of pre-planning
- It was a sophisticated offence

- The offence deliberately targeted the vulnerable
- The offenders operated as part of a group or gang
- A high level of gain from the offence
- High value (including sentimental value) of property to victim or substantial consequential loss.

Mitigating factors taken into account when sentencing:

- The property has been returned undamaged
- Impact on sentence of offender's dependency - dependency does not mitigate seriousness of offence but may properly influence type of sentence imposed
- The offender was motivated by desperation or need (in exceptional circumstances)

CPS Guidelines on prosecution for theft from shop or stall

Aggravating factors taken into account when sentencing:

- *Child accompanying offender is involved in or aware of theft*
- *Offender is subject to a banning order that includes the store*

- *Offender motivated by intention to cause harm or revenge*
- *Professional offending*
- *Victim particularly vulnerable (e.g. small independent shop)*
- *Offender targeted high value goods.*

CPS Sentencing guidelines

First time offender aged 18 or over who pleaded not guilty:

- *No Planning or sophistication and low value = Starting point fine to Conditional Discharge or low level fine.*
- *Low level intimidation or threat or some planning e.g. session on the same day or going equipped or some relevant damage = Low level Community Order or Medium*

Community Order.

- *Significant intimidation or threats or use force resulting in slight injury or very high level planning or significant relevant damage = 6 weeks imprisonment or High level (36 weeks) Community Order.*

- *Vulnerable victims involving and intimidation or threat of force = Starting point of 12 months imprisonment and/or Ancillary Orders available such as Restitution, Compensation, Deprivation, and POCA.*

ROBBERY

Indictable offence.

Maximum sentence = Life imprisonment

Robbery is a form of 'aggravated theft' and comes under Section 8 of the Theft Act (1968). Before the establishment of the Theft Act, robbery was a common law offence (considered illegal through the decisions of previous judges) and was described as:

"Robbery is the felonious and violent taking of any money or goods from the person of another, putting him in fear, be the value thereof above or under one shilling"

Nowadays Robbery is a little more defined through the Acts of Parliament and Section 8 now makes Robbery an offence when:

"A person is guilty of robbery if he steals, and immediately before or at the time of doing so, and in order to do so, he uses force on any person or puts any person in fear of being then and there subjected to force".

Robbery comes under Section 8 of the Theft Act (1968). It is a more serious form of theft and is an indictable offence (meaning that it can be tried only in the Crown Court) unlike theft which can be tried in either a Magistrates' or Crown Court. The seriousness of robbery is also reflected in its maximum sentence of life imprisonment as opposed to only seven years for theft.

So what is robbery? Well, to put it simply, robbery is theft with the **immediate** use of force, or theft involving putting, or seeking to put, a person in fear of **immediate** force. The force (or threat of force) must be immediately before or at the time of the theft. Not afterwards. If it were afterwards the defendant could be charged with theft and assault but not robbery. The intended victim of the force does not necessarily have to be the victim of the theft. They can be two separate persons, however the victim of the force must be aware that they are being assaulted or threatened with the use of force in order to steal.

Threats of force

Section 8 of the Theft Act makes it clear that actual force does not necessarily have to be used. If the offender puts a person in fear of being 'then and there' subjected to force (or if the offender seeks to put the victim in fear of being subjected to force) then that will suffice.

Notice the word 'immediately'?

The force used, threatened or put upon the victim by the offender must be immediate. If it is not then a charge of theft accompanied by a separate charge of assault may be used, but not robbery.

So how could we define immediate? Well the use of force must be immediately before or at the time of the theft and the definition of 'immediate' in robbery is not so straightforward. If we take, for example, a scenario whereby the offender approaches the bank manager on his way to work. The offender tells the bank manager that he will assault him if he does not go to the bank and put all the cash in a bag so the offender can collect it in 20 minutes. Would this be Robbery according to section 8?

No. The threat of force and the actual theft have not occurred immediately together and so there is no robbery. It would more likely be two separate charges… one of theft and one of blackmail in this case.

Now let us take another scenario whereby the offender approaches the bank manager, assaults him, or threatens force, and takes the bag full of cash at the same time?

Yes, this would be robbery as the force was used immediately before/during the theft.

There is no set time limit to define 'immediate' within the scope of robbery. Ultimately it would be for the jury in the trial to decide upon whether the time period between the two acts could be considered then and there 'immediate' but, as a general rule, the longer the time period between the two acts the less chance there is of robbery.

The use/threat of force in order to steal

The use or threat of force must be in order to accomplish the task of theft. So if the offender punches the victim to the ground in order to steal his wallet, then we would have robbery. If the offender punches the victim to the ground because he does not like them, and then sees the wallet and decides to take it, then we would not have robbery but instead two charges, one of theft and one of assault. This is because the intention of the force used was not in order to commit the theft.

What defines force?

Again this is not straightforward. In some cases it would be obvious (for example where the thief uses a gun to threaten the victim in order to get what they want. This would more than likely be enough to constitute force and so robbery. But what about the offender that runs past a victim, snatching their mobile phone and runs off with it? What if they pushed the victim over as they snatched the phone? This would not be so straight forward and often depends upon a number of factors including whether the victim is hurt or if the victim put up a struggle or believed they were going to be assaulted if they did not give the offender what they wanted. Ultimately it would be for the jury to decide whether enough force was used to constitute robbery. If it is decided that not enough force is used then the charge would remain as section 1, 'Theft'.

The awareness of force

As we have already observed, actual force is not necessary. The threat of force is enough. So long as the victim is aware that force is being used, or will be used, or the intention of the offender was to put the victim in fear of force.

The threat does not have to be direct either. So the offender does not necessarily have to say "I will assault you if you do not give me your wallet". If the offender makes a veiled threat such as "Give me your wallet or else" and the victim understands this to be a threat of force then that will suffice.

So what if the threat of force is used against one person in order to steal from another?

Well now we have two separate victims. It would still constitute robbery so long as the person to whom the threat is made is aware of the threat and that it is in order to commit the theft.

So as an example, the offender approaches the victim and says "give me your wallet or I will hurt your friend sat over there". Now, if the friend sat by the way hears this and is aware of the threat and theft then we would have robbery. But, if the friend is too far away to hear and is completely unaware then we would not have robbery because the victim of force is not aware.

The robbery is unsuccessful?

Section 8(2) of the Theft Act (1968) creates the offence of "Assault with intent to rob". This means that where the robbery fails and the offender does not get around to demanding the property or money (perhaps they have been arrested before they get the opportunity) but they had the intention to commit a robbery, then they can still be charged with this offence instead of section 8(1) 'Robbery'. Both offences are indictable and carry maximum sentences of life imprisonment.

Burglary

Indictable offence

Maximum sentence = 14 years

"A person is guilty of burglary if:

(a) he enters any building or part of a building as a trespasser and with intent to commit any such offence as is mentioned in subsection (2) below; or

(b) having entered any building or part of a building as a trespasser he steals or attempts to steal anything in the building or that part of it or inflicts or attempts to inflict on any person therein any grievous bodily harm."

A person commits burglary when he or she enters a building, or a part of a building, as a trespasser, and they either commit, or intend to commit, a theft or to inflict a grievous bodily harm against a person or to cause unlawful damage.

Burglary is an offence under section 9 of the Theft Act (1968) and prosecutions come under two subsections of this. Sections 9(1)(a) and 9(1)(b). These two subsections differ as to how far the burglary has gone...

Section 9(1)(a) or Section 9(1)(b)?

Section 9(1)(a) is used if the offender:

1) Enters a building (or any part of a building)

2) As a trespasser

3) With the intention of committing the act of theft, a criminal damage or grievous bodily harm (or any combination of the three).

Section 9(1)(b) is used if the offender:

1) Enter a building (or any part of a building)

2) As a trespasser

3) And commits the act of theft, a criminal damage or grievous bodily harm (or any

combination of the three).

So should the offender enter a building with the intention of committing theft and they are caught in the process then they would have committed an offence under section 9(1)(a) because they have not committed the theft, only intended on doing so. If they entered the building, stole property, got away and then were apprehended later then the offence would be section 9(1)(b). The terms of punishment available to the courts are the same for both offences so in effect it matters not whether the offender got away at the time or not, so long as they entered the building as a trespasser.

Enters

Quite straight forward to start off with. The offender puts himself inside the property.

The thief that steals through an open window

So what if the offender does not actually enter the building but instead reaches through the open window to take the property? In effect only part of him or her has trespassed so would this still be entry?

Well this is another open decision. There is no set percentage of the person's body which has to enter the property to constitute entry to the building but previous case law (decisions of the courts and jury in similar trials) have stated that 'yes', this would still constitute entry to the premises for the purpose of burglary even if only a part of the offenders body has technically entered. The final decision would however be made by the jury in that particular case.

But what about those offenders that do not physically enter the building at all, but instead use a tool or implement? For example the offender that sticks the fishing line through a letterbox to retrieve the car keys inside a house? Have they still affected entry to the property?

Again this is another open decision. It could be argued that the fishing line is effectively an extension of the offender's body, modified because the offender's arms were too thick to go through the letter box or not long enough to reach the car keys. A jury could go either way in reaching a decision as to whether the charge is burglary or simple theft.

Building, or part of

Building is not defined within the Theft Act or, more specifically, with section 9 'Burglary'. This means that it is within the scope of the courts and the jury to determine whether the property entered by the offender would in fact be 'a building' for the purposes of burglary. Generally, however, it would be down to common sense what is a building (or part of a building).

Section 9(4) does make clear that an inhabited vehicle or vessel is a building for the purposes of burglary. This means that a house boat or motor home/caravan would be considered a building when it is being used.

So, if you own a caravan which you use for two weeks in July and during those two weeks it is broken into, then we would have a burglary. This is because at the time of the trespass/entry/theft it is an inhabited vehicle and so a dwelling and as such 'a building'. However, if it is broken into on the third day of February when it is sat in your drive way and unused then it would not be considered a dwelling for the purposes of burglary and as such not a building.

'Or part of a building' is also up for negotiation. The purpose of 'or part of a building' is to cover where an offender may argue that they have not entirely entered the building and only a part of it (such as an outhouse or garage). This way it would still be covered under the Act. It is worth noting that there is a wider scope to this however. Where a person enters a shop they have the permission of the owner to browse the shop floor, try on clothes in the changing rooms, or perhaps go into the restaurant to drink a coffee. These are all areas of the property where permission is given. But if the offender goes behind the till point and, for example, steals the contents of the tills or enters a restricted stock room out back to steal, then they have entered a part of the building where they do not have permission to be. This would be trespassing in a part of the building with theft, and as such would be a burglary.

Trespasser

The offender has entered the property without the consent of its owner or 'guardian' is trespassing. The offender does not need to have entered on purpose. If they were reckless as to entering the property then this is also trespassing.

Intention

An intention to commit either theft, unlawful damage, or GBH is essential to the offence of burglary. The offender must have intended to trespass in order to commit one of these offences for the offence to be complete. It does not matter if the offender had no specific intention. It could be that they would enter the premises as a trespasser to have a look around and then decide if there was anything worth stealing, damaging or destroying. The fact that the offender has contemplated these actions when they trespassed is enough to qualify them for burglary as the contemplation is also an intention.

The offender that lies in order to gain entry

If an offender gives an untrue story in order to gain access to the property, are they still a trespasser? They could have said they were there to read the gas meter and so been allowed onto the premises in which case they have been given permission to enter.

There is nothing in the Theft Act (1968) to suggest that fraudulently gaining access to a premises would be trespass, however previous case law and statements given by the judiciary and legal scholars (the words of judges and other legal authorities can be used as persuasive argument when deciding upon cases) suggests that deceptively gaining access to property is still trespass as the 'true' permission has not been given by the owner. This means that it is probable that trespass for the purposes of burglary would also include where the offender has been untrue in their intentions.

Exceeding the permission of the property owner

When a person enters a property under the permission of the owner there is an expectation of what they can do whilst they are there. So, for example, a person renting a room in a house has the permission of the owner to live in the house, cook their food in the kitchen, wash in the shower, etc., etc... When a person enters a shop, they have the permission of the shop's owner to browse the goods for sale, purchase items, use the stores coffee shop, etc., etc... Now if the person renting the room stole personal property not belonging to them or the person entering the shop set the display on fire then they would have exceeded the permission of the owner as the owner will undoubtedly not have given permission, or probably even expected that behavior. If the owners had known prior they would no doubt have refused any permission to enter their property.

Previous case law has stated that where a person has permission to enter a property for lawful purposes and then has entered for an unlawful purpose which not permission has been given for then this could amount to trespass for the purposes of burglary.

It is worth noting that this would technically make virtually all offences of shoplifting into burglary as the shoplifter has exceeded the terms of their entering the store. However, in reality it would be very rare for a shoplifter to be prosecuted for burglary as proving simple theft from a shop or stall is far simpler and time effective.

Theft from a shop when the offender is banned

Security Officers working in large stores will undoubtedly have come across persistent offenders that have been banned from the shop in question. When the offender is banned then any permission given to them to enter the premises has been withdrawn and so trespass occurs when they enter. If they then commit a theft, for example, we have a burglary.

The problem here occurs in proving that the offender was banned from the store. Because of the risk of a failed prosecution when the offender claims to have not been banned or not received any form of banning notice, the prosecution services will 9 times out of 10 only prosecute for Theft and not for Burglary. However, when arresting or making a complaint against an offender that is banned from your premises your statement should always include the details of the offenders ban (such as when they were banned, how they were banned, and by whom). This not only allows the prosecution services the 'option' to charge with Burglary but the Magistrate or Judge may impose a higher sentence for the Theft or Burglary (whichever is used) with the aggravating factor that they were trespassing.

AGGRAVATED BURGLARY

<u>Indictable offence</u>

<u>Maximum sentence = life imprisonment</u>

"A person is guilty of aggravated burglary if he commits any burglary and at the time has with him any firearm or imitation firearm, any weapon of offence, or any explosive"

Aggravated burglary is a far more serious offence than 'burglary' and offenders found guilty of aggravated burglary generally are given far harsher penalties than those found guilty of burglary. This is reflected in its maximum sentence of life imprisonment

<u>So what make a burglary 'aggravated'?</u>

To commit the offence of burglary, remember that, the offender must have entered a property, as a trespasser, with the intention to (or reckless as to) steal, unlawfully damage or inflict grievous bodily harm on another person. To make the offence that of section 10 "Aggravated Burglary", the offender must have committed the same act with the same intention, but at the time of the act they had with them any firearm, explosive or any other weapon of offence. It does not matter that the firearm, explosive or other weapon may not have been 'carried' with the intention of using them for the burglary. The fact that the offender 'had with him at the time' is enough to satisfy the requirements of aggravated burglary.

The mere use of force is not enough to constitute aggravated burglary so the offender that assaults a person in the course of a burglary will not be considered to have committed aggravated burglary. This is a common misconception. The offender must have with them the "weapon of offence".

Firearm, explosive or other weapon of offence

These terms have a very broad definition when looked at closely, but section 10(1)(a),(b), & (c) give accurate definitions of what would come under these description.

Firearm

Firearm or imitation firearm includes of course your general bullet firing AK47's and Glock 9mm as well as pellet firing air guns or air rifles. It matters not whether the 'firearm' is powerful. It is still a firearm. An imitation firearm is exactly as it describes... anything with the appearance of a firearm. Whether this is a plastic toy or deactivated gun or a banana in the coat pocket used to give a physical impression of a firearm.

Explosive

An explosive is anything which can, or has been intended to, explode. Even if it is faulty and will not actually explode, if the person carrying it has the intention of it being used as an explosive then it is an explosive.

Weapon of offence

A weapon of offence is anything which was made for causing injury or incapacitating another person (such as a knife) or anything which has been adapted to cause injury or incapacitating another person (such as a snooker ball in a sock – separately they are harmless items but when the ball is put in the sock it becomes a cosh which can be used to injure and so is an improvised weapon of offence). Weapon of offence includes anything, intended by the person having it, which will cause harm regardless of whether it is actually capable of doing so. This means that if the item carried by the offender is intended to stab another person but is in fact so blunt that it would not pierce a sheet of paper it will still be considered a weapon of offence regardless of the fact it is incapable. The fact that the carrier intended the weapon for this is enough to class it as offensive.

REMOVAL OF ARTICLES FROM PLACES OPEN TO THE PUBLIC

<u>Indictable offence</u>

<u>Maximum term = 5 years</u>

"any person who without lawful authority removes from the building or its grounds the whole or part of any article displayed or kept for display to the public in the building or that part of it or in its grounds shall be guilty of an offence"

So as we have already seen a burglary requires a person to enter a building (or part of a building) as a trespasser with the intention of stealing, causing unlawful damage or committing a grievous bodily harm. But what if the person committing the theft is fully entitled to be inside the building because it is open to the public? They are no longer trespassing and so could not possibly be committing a burglary because that important factor is missing. As we already know from theft, it could be considered that the offender has surpassed the permission given to them by stealing (as a person's permission to enter a museum, for example, would not include stealing the exhibits) and so they would then be trespassing by exceeding the permission given them. This, however, is not an easy thing to prove. There are very few convictions based upon the idea of exceeding or breaching the permission given in order to prove trespass especially where the permission given is not directly put upon the offender but is a general allowance for all persons to enter the premises or property. It is for this reason that we have Section 11 of the Theft Act (1968) the 'removal of articles from places open to the public'. Section 11 creates an offence whereby a person that has legal permission, by way of general entry by the public in order to view the building or a collection within the building, commits an offence if they remove any part of the building or item displayed in it. It also covers where the item is kept in the building for display to the public on a later occasion.

The building includes:

The physical property itself (such as house, gallery or museum) and the grounds to which it belongs (so it's gardens or outhouses).

Collection includes:

Any items (whether temporarily or permanently) put together for view by the public. This would not include any items which were made or exhibited to the public in order to sell or promote anything commercial (so section 11 would cover where a person, for example, takes a display vase from a museum exhibition where the vase is for view by the public but it would not cover the theft of the same vase if it were on display in an auction house where it would be for sale).

Time period

To fulfill the requirements of this offence the offender must commit the theft on a day that the premises are open to the public. So if the offender steals a painting from the museum on the day the museum is open he will have committed an offence of section 11 'removal of articles from places open to the public'. However if, for example, it is Christmas day and the museum is closed then the offender would not have permission to enter the building anyway so then we would revert to the original offence of burglary as he or she would also have committed a trespass.

Defense

As with theft, the offender must have been dishonest in their actions so if the person believed that they had a lawful right to remove the item or items then theft would not have been committed and so neither would the removal of articles from places open to the public.

TAKING A MOTOR VEHICLE OR OTHER CONVEYANCE WITHOUT AUTHORITY

Summary offence

Maximum penalty = Level 5 fine and/or 6 months imprisonment

"without having the consent of the owner or other lawful authority, he takes any conveyance for his own or another's use or, knowing that any conveyance has been taken without such authority, drives it or allows his self to be carried in or on it"

The title says it all really… If a person takes a motor vehicle, or other conveyance, without the permission and consent of its owner, or controller, then they will have committed an offence under section 12 of the Theft Act (1968), so long as they have either:

1. taken the vehicle for their own or another's use, or
2. they drive it, or
3. they allow themselves to be carried in it, knowing that the vehicle has been taken without consent

It is important to note point 3 above because it means that the offence applies not only to the person taking the vehicle but also to the passengers in the vehicle (so long as they knew the vehicle had been taken without the owner's consent).

The requirements of the act of theft require that a person permanently deprive another person of their property. In the past, offenders have taken a motor vehicle with the intention of 'joyriding' in it. This meant that there was no intention to permanently deprive as the 'joyrider' would simply abandon the vehicle when they had finished with it, which would naturally mean the 'owner' would get it back, and so it would be argued that the offender was innocent of theft because they were only 'borrowing' without permission. This made convictions rather uncertain and an offence difficult to prove. For this reason came Section 12 'Taking a motor vehicle or other conveyance without authority'. If a jury were uncertain that the offender had committed an act of theft, the option is available to find them guilty of taking a motor vehicle or other conveyance without authority.

The Conveyance

Section 12(7)(a) of the Theft Act (1968) determines what is meant by 'conveyance'. It means anything which is constructed, or has been adapted, for the carriage of a person or persons whether by land, water or air. So a car or motorcycle are things constructed for the carriage of people across land and would be covered. A boat would be the same by sea and a plane by air. All of these would be covered by section 12.

But what about an unmanned aircraft I hear you say? Well no. The conveyance must be used to carry the person, not just <u>be</u> under the control of a person. So an unmanned aircraft (like the ones used by the military) would not be covered as although a person is controlling it, they are not being carried in it at the time. Likewise a radio controlled model car could in theory be considered a vehicle. It has a motor (electric or petrol) and it drives. But the person controlling it is not being carried in it. They are stood nearby controlling it so again this would not be covered by section 12.

Man powered conveyances

Non-motorized conveyances such as bicycles are also covered by section 12(5) of the Theft Act (1968), however the maximum penalties are lower. So a person that takes a pedal powered bicycle may also be committing the offence of taking a motor vehicle or other conveyance without authority but the maximum penalty imposed can only be a level 3 fine.

AGGRAVATED VEHICLE TAKING

Triable either way

Maximum penalty = 14 years imprisonment

"at any time after the vehicle was unlawfully taken (whether by him or another) and before it was recovered, the vehicle was driven, or injury or damage was caused"

Section 12A of the Theft Act (1968) is an extension of the offence previously given of section 12 'taking a motor vehicle or other conveyance without authority'. Section 12A is a more serious form however and is triable in the Crown courts rather than Magistrates' courts. The maximum sentence that can be imposed is four times that of section 12.

So if a person removes or takes a motor vehicle, or other conveyance, without the permission and consent of its owner, or controller, then they will have committed an offence under section 12 of the Theft Act (1968) 'taking a motor vehicle or other conveyance without authority', so long as they have either:

1. taken the vehicle for their own or another's use, or
2. they drive it, or
3. they allow themselves to be carried in it, knowing that the vehicle has been taken without consent

For section 12A to apply then, as well as the previous criteria, the offender must also have, at some point between taking the vehicle and the owner recovering the vehicle, either:

1. driven the vehicle dangerously on a road or other public place ('dangerously' according to the courts would mean driven in a way which falls far below what would be expected of a competent and careful driver and in a manner which would be obvious to a competent and careful driver as being dangerous), or

2. that by driving the vehicle an accident occurred which either injured a person or damaged property, or damaged the vehicle itself.

Culpability

Maximum sentences imposed for section 12a Aggravated vehicle taking are dependent upon the outcome of the offence and can range from maximums of 2 years to 14 years. The more serious end of the spectrum (causing death or injury as a result of the offence obviously attracts the higher sentence whilst damage to property the lower).

ABSTRACTING OF ELECTRICITY

<u>Indictable offence</u>

<u>Maximum penalty – 5 years imprisonment</u>

"A person who dishonestly uses without due authority, or dishonestly causes to be wasted or diverted, any electricity shall on conviction on indictment be liable to imprisonment for a term not exceeding five years"

The abstracting of electricity is covered by section 13 of the Theft Act (1968). It creates an offence when a person dishonestly and without authority, causes any electricity to be wasted or diverted. Now this does not mean that when you 'waste electric' by leaving the light switch on you face up to 5 years in prison. The abstracting of electricity must be sufficiently serious to warrant a prosecution and must be within the public interest.

Generally this offence is used where a person 'steals' electricity by using what is known as a 'black box' to 'adjust' the reading on an electric meter resulting in them paying for less electric. The offence is considered more serious, and will attract the higher sentence, where there is pre-planning of the offence, there is a high value loss, the abstraction creates a danger to property or life, or the abstraction is to facilitate another offence (such as cultivating cannabis).

Joyriding in a lift

Here we have a very common past time in retail stores often referred to as 'Joyriding in a lift'. Lifts are provided in buildings to carry their passengers from floor to floor. Most often in retail stores they are for the convenience of the stores customers or for the disabled to use to give easier access to the different levels of the store. Specifically the lifts are in place for those reasons and the lift uses electrical energy to move. This electrical energy is paid for by the store that has them. If we take an example where a group of juveniles get in the lift and use it to go up and down the levels of the store with no intention other than to 'enjoy the ride' then they are not using the lift (or the electric) for the purpose it has been intended. This would be wasting electric and so 'technically' an offence under section 13.

Please note, however, that although 'joyriding in a

lift' is technically an offence under section 13, the public interest in stopping this unwanted juvenile activity is very, very, low. In fact I would go as far as saying that there would be no public interest and so an arrest or complaint made against juveniles committing this would not be recommended and should be read as 'interest only'.

HANDLING STOLEN GOODS

<u>Triable either-way offence</u>

<u>Maximum penalty = 14 years</u>

"A person handles stolen goods if (otherwise than in the course of the stealing) knowing or believing them to be stolen goods he dishonestly receives the goods, or dishonestly undertakes or assists in their retention, removal, disposal or realization by or for the benefit of another person, or if he arranges to do so"

Section 22 of the Theft Act (1968) creates an offence of handling stolen goods. The offender 'handles the stolen goods' if he dishonestly receives the goods or undertakes or assists in the retention, removal, disposal or realization of those goods.

The stolen goods

The stolen goods being handled is the same as the property stolen in the act of theft. So any item of property which can, by law, be stolen (with regards the theft under the Theft Act (1968) (so tangible and non-tangible items, animals kept in captivity, etc...)) can later be handled.

The definition of stolen goods under section 22 is further reaching however. 'Stolen goods' can also include the proceeds of such theft or anything brought with those proceeds. So if the thief (Mr. A) steals an antique vase and then sells it to Mr. B for £500 and then Mr. A gives that £500 to Mr. C to look after, then Mr. C will be guilty of handling stolen goods (provided he knew, or thought possible, that the £500 was the proceeds from the stolen vase. Likewise if Mr. A (the thief) brought a new car with the £500 and gave it to Mr. C to look after then Mr. C again would be guilty of handling stolen goods, irrespective of the fact that he has at no point come into contact with the original stolen vase.

Receiving

Takes delivery of the goods or takes the goods from

another person.

Retention

Holds the goods for another person (whether permanently or temporarily)

Removal

Takes the goods away.

Disposal

Takes possession of the goods in order to discard/dump/throw them away.

Realization

Converts the goods by way of selling them or turning them into something else

The handler

Now for the offence to be complete, the handler of the goods must know, or believe, the goods to be stolen. The handler does not necessarily have to be certain that they are stolen. If he or she even believes that the goods might be stolen then they will have still committed the offence of handling stolen goods.

So how would the courts know that the defendant believed the goods to be stolen, or may be stolen? Well there is such a thing as a "willful blindness to the circumstances". In other words…"don't be ridiculous". The courts understand that if the defendant brought the property "off a bloke in the pub" for a fraction of its real value then to any normal person we would have an inkling that there was something "dodgy" about the transaction This would mean that the defendant would also have realized the same thing and so the excuse of "I didn't know they were stolen when I brought them off the bloke, who I don't know, in the dark alley way" is not credible in a court.

Handling stolen goods does not cover the receiving, retention, removal, disposal or realization of the goods in the course of the stealing. So if we have two shoplifters. One selects the goods and walks out of the shop door with them and the second receives the goods outside and walks away with them, we do not have one offence of theft and one offence of handling stolen goods because both offenders have 'handled the goods in the course of stealing them'. If we have one shoplifter that steals the goods and then he catches the bus to his friend's house where he gives the goods to his friend then we would have one offence of theft (the shoplifter) and one offence of handling stolen goods (the friend).

ADVERTISING REWARDS FOR GOODS LOST OR STOLEN

<u>Summary offence</u>

<u>Maximum sentence = Level 3 fine</u>

"Where any public advertisement of a reward for the return of any goods which have been stolen or lost uses any words to the effect that no questions will be asked, or that the person producing the goods will be safe from apprehension or inquiry, or that any money paid for the purchase of the goods or advanced by way of loan on them will be repaid, the person advertising the reward and any person who prints or publishes the advertisement shall on summary conviction be liable"

Section 23 of the Theft Act (1968) makes an offence of advertising, printing or publishing a reward for goods lost or stolen if the advertisement implies or suggests that the person producing the goods will be safe from apprehension or inquiry by the authorities or that any money the 'finder' paid for the lost goods will be returned to them.

This means that a person advertising a 'finder's reward'

of, for example, £5 for their lost phone is perfectly entitled to do so. However, a person cannot advertise a £5 reward for their lost or stolen phone and advertise that the finder will not be spoken to by the police or that they will be immune from any prosecution if they do so.

Advertising

This does not necessarily mean taking out a center page advertisement in the local paper. A person is still advertising if they spread the information by word of mouth or by putting up posters on lampposts in the local area. Anything which would imply from one person to another could be considered an advertisement.

The guilty party

This does not necessarily have to be the person stating the proposal. The person making the advertisement (such as a printer if they are on posters) will also be guilty of the same offence.

GOING EQUIPPED FOR STEALING

Indictable offence

Maximum penalty = 3 years imprisonment

Section 25 of the Theft Act (1968) creates the offence of 'going equipped to steal'. This means that any person that has with him, or her, any article (when they are not at their place of abode) which can be used for the purpose of a burglary or theft (or in connection with a burglary or theft) is committing an offence.

Articles

The term 'articles' is not specific within section 25 and so it would be for the courts and the jury to decide if such an 'article' could be used for the purpose of a theft or burglary, however, generally the term 'article' would be items such as 'crowbars' and 'hacksaws' for burglaries or 'handcuffs' and 'ammonia spray' for use in robberies. The list of possible 'articles' is endless.

Connection with

The article must be connected to the specific offence the offender is believed to be carrying it for. So if it is believed the offender is going to commit a burglary the article in question may be a lock pick. If the offender is carrying a piece of paper, then there may be some question as to how that could be used to commit a burglary.

Place of abode

'Place of abode' means a residence of the person holding the article. It must be a place of abode at the time it was found. So if the offender lives in a caravan and has a set of lock picks in the caravan then they are at his place of abode and so not within the scope of section 25. However, if the caravan is being towed to a new location then it is no longer a place of abode because it is in transit.

Before or after the theft/burglary

Previous case law has shown that the offender does not necessarily have to have the article in his possession before the crime is committed. The offender can still be charged with 'going equipped' even if they have already committed the apparent offence and are in fact 'going home equipped to steal'.

Burden of proof

It is the duty of the prosecution to prove beyond reasonable doubt that the article found is connected to the relevant offence being, or which has been, committed. So it would not be enough to claim that the screwdriver found in the defendants pocket is for the use in a burglary. The prosecution will have to prove that it was intended for the use in a burglary and not to tighten the screws on the defendant's kitchen cabinets.

MAKING OFF WITHOUT PAYMENT

<u>Triable either-way</u>

<u>Maximum penalty = 2 years imprisonment</u>

The Theft Act (1968) created the offence of 'Theft'. However, there is sometimes difficulty in securing a conviction for these offences where the defendant denies that they never had an intention to pay. If a person fills their car with petrol and then drives off without paying, how can it be proved that they were not planning on returning later to pay for the fuel?

This is where Section 3(1) of the Theft Act (1978) comes in. It creates an offence the moment the offender 'makes off' and the questions of when the intention not to pay was formed and when control of the property was passed from one person to another are irrelevant. The offence only requires that:

Goods were supplied to the offender or a service was performed, and

These goods or service required payment or payment was expected, and

The offender made off from the spot that payment was required, and

The offender knew that payment was required, and

The offender intended to avoid payment permanently, and

The offender was dishonest in his actions.

Goods supplied or a service performed

The offender had to have obtained some form of goods (such as petrol or a meal) or had a service performed (such as a car wash).

Payment was required or expected

The offender was supposed to have made payment for the goods or the service.

From the spot that payment was required

This does not literally have to be a 'spot'. The area that payment is required can be a large area. "On the spot" means a payment <u>at the time</u> of collecting the goods or in respect of the service performed.

Knew that payment was required

If the offender had a meal in a restaurant then it could safely be assumed that they knew that payment would be required afterwards.

Intended to avoid payment

The offender must have had an intention not to pay. If they had informed the restaurant staff, for example, that they were going to the bank to get some money and would return to make payment then they would not have an intention to avoid payment.

Dishonesty

Again it must be shown that the offender was dishonest. This would be for the jury and the courts to decide upon in order to determine guilt.

Illegal and immoral services

Making off without payment cannot be an offence if the service provided was illegal or unenforceable by law (section 3(1) TA.1978). So, for example, a person making off without payment for services from a prostitute would not be liable for this offence because the service provided was illegal. (It could be noted, however, that a person making off without payment for services from a prostitute may still be liable for Section 1 of the Fraud Act 2006, Fraud by false representation').

Fraud

The Fraud Act 2006

The Fraud Act of 2006 was introduced to overhaul and simplify the previous offences of deception which came under the Theft Act 1968 and which were previously rather difficult to prove. The Fraud Act also further clarified the offence of fraud.

Fraud is one of the fastest increasing offences in the United Kingdom, mainly due to the increased use of distance banking and shopping. It is estimated that in the United Kingdom alone fraud cost the British economy almost £40 billion per year. Many of us will have been the victims of fraud at some stage or at least know someone who has been.

Triable either-way offence

Maximum penalty = A fine and/or up to 12 months imprisonment on summary conviction or a fine and/or up to 10 years imprisonment on conviction on indictment.

So what is Fraud?

Fraud is a form of deception used to gain property or money for oneself or to create a loss for the victim. The money or form of property gained or the loss caused to the victim does not necessarily have to be permanent. The offender may only intend the loss or gain to be temporary. Even so, it would still be an offence of fraud. The Fraud Act 2006 defines fraud as being an offence based upon dishonesty and can be committed in three different ways:

1. Fraud by false representation
2. fraud by failing to disclose information
3. Fraud by abuse of position

It is quite common for offenders found guilty of fraud, as well as receiving up to 10 years imprisonment and/or a fine, to receive other forms of punishment or retribution including 'Compensation orders', 'Deprivation orders' and 'Disqualification from acting as a company director'.

The level of punishment imposed will often depend on a number of factors including the amount in involved in the fraud, what the money was used for (for example a person using the victims money to fund a lavish life style would more than likely receive a larger penalty than those that gave it charity), if the victim was elderly or in some way more vulnerable, whether the offender was in a position of trust as well as many other factors.

1. Fraud by False Representation

Fraud by false representation comes under section 2 of the Fraud Act 2006 and a person is guilty of fraud by false representation when they commit a fraud by making a representation (statement) which they know to be untrue.

For an offender to be guilty of fraud by false representation under section 2 of the Fraud Act 2006 they must:

- make a representation that is false (i.e. they must perform some sort of conduct which is untrue or misleading), and

- know that their representation is, or might be, untrue or misleading, and

- must be dishonest in their representation, and

- must intend to make some sort of gain for themselves or another person, or intend to cause or expose the victim to a loss (the gain can be of money or property whether tangible or intangible (remember things you can touch are tangible and those you cannot, such as credit card numbers and bank balances, are intangible)), and

- the representation may be express or implied (the offender may specifically state the false conduct or imply it be leading the victim to believe them)

Not really false??

So the offender attempts to make a false representation by selling a 2 carat diamond ring to the victim by claiming the ring is in fact 20 carats. Their we have a false representation because the fraudster has made a false statement to the victim in order that they make a gain (of the money paid for the ring). They know the representation to be untrue and misleading and have indeed done so dishonestly. But what if it transpires that the offender is mistaken, and all along the diamond ring was in fact 20 carats? Does the offence still exist?

No. There would be no false representation as they have not made a representation that is false (the first requirement on the list) as it has turned out that what the offender has said is true. It does not matter that their intention was to give a false statement if the statement is in fact true. But… the offender has still attempted to commit the offence and so could be liable for attempting to commit fraud by false representation under the Criminal Attempts Act which we shall look at later.

The victim is not stupid?

So the offender attempts to sell a 2 carat ring claiming it to be 20 carats. This time the ring really is 2 carats and the person who is being targeted knows it is 2 carats. Still an offence?

Yes. Just because the victim has not fallen for it and the offender has not been successful does not mean there is no offence. The offender has still committed Fraud by False Representation and the offence was complete the moment he or she made the false statement.

False representation to a machine

The offender is still guilty of the same offence regardless of whether they were 'cheating' a human or a machine. So we would still have fraud by false representation if the offender attempted to commit the offence against a 'self-checkout' machine, by inserting an invalid credit card for example, as we would if they had committed an offence against a human sales person on the till point.

2. Fraud by failing to disclose information

Fraud by failing to disclose information is an offence under section 3 of the Fraud Act 2006. It is committed when a person fails to disclose information when they are under a legal duty to do so and in order to make a gain or cause loss.

For an offender to be guilty of Fraud by failing to disclose information they must:

- withhold information
- their must be a legal obligation not to withhold that specific information
- the information must have been withheld dishonestly and not just through mistake
- the offender must have done so in order to make a gain for himself or another person, or in order

to cause a loss to the victim

So when is there a legal obligation to disclose information?

There are occasions when a legal obligation to disclose all necessary information is required. These can be where there is some form of contract, such as an insurance agreement or a sale of goods, or where there is a legal obligation enforced by a specific law such as an Act of Parliament. In fact, pretty much any situation where information will be exchanged before a formal decision is made will require all necessary information to be divulged.

3. Fraud by abuse of position

This is defined by section 4 of the Fraud Act 2006 and is committed when a person that is employed or occupies a position where they are expected to safeguard the financial interests of another person, and they abuse that position either by failing to do an act expected of them or by doing an act which creates the gain for themselves/another or causes a loss to the victim.

A person commits this offence when they:

- occupy a position of which they are expected to safeguard, or not to act against, the financial interests of another person
- they dishonestly abuse that position
- by doing so they intend to make a gain for

themselves or another person, or create a loss to the victim

S.6 Possession of articles for use in fraud

Section 6 of the Fraud Act 2006 also creates the offence of having in possession, or control, articles or an article for use in fraud. This means that the offender can face up to five years imprisonment without necessarily having to attempt or commit the fraud so long as the article in question has been obtained for use in fraud or the offender plans on using it for such.

'Articles' under section 6 is not specific and the list of so called articles which can be used is almost limitless. However, the most common article used in modern days is the computer. So if the offender has a computer with the intention of using that for fraudulent activity then it would not be necessary to wait for the offender to use it for that purpose before they are arrestable/prosecutable. Articles can also mean the software or information stored on a computer even though that information or software is intangible.

S.11 Obtaining services dishonestly

Section 11 of the Fraud Act 2006 creates a further offence of Obtaining services dishonestly. The difference between section 11 and other fraud offences is that the offender has obtained a 'service' as a result of their fraud rather than money or property. The offender must have had the knowledge or intention that no payment would be made.

This offence could apply to any number of scenarios but could be anything from a person obtaining thousands of pounds in building work on a property knowing that they are unable to pay when it is finished to a person riding on the bus or train without paying.

To commit this offence

To commit this offence the offender must:

- obtain a service, or services, for himself, or another, and

- been dishonest at the time of doing so, and

- obtained the service on the understanding or belief that payment would be made for it, and

- intend not to make payment for the service given.

Defences against the offence

A person is not guilty of Obtaining services dishonestly if he or she:

- honestly believed, when they obtained the services, that they would pay for them, even if they did not have the money at the time but believed that later they would have it, or

- simply forgot to pay for the services,

- where their is a genuine dispute over the services done (such as the 'payer' believes the service is of an unworthy standard), or
- was offered the service for free (even if they were dishonest in obtaining that service, such as the opening of a bank account if the bank account was free to open).

THE GUARD DOGS ACT (1975)

<u>Summary offence</u>

<u>Maximum sentence = Level 5 fine</u>

The Guard Dogs Act (1975) was introduced to regulate the use of guard dogs within private security. It is relatively simple legislation dealing with the control of guard dogs when they are with and without their handler as well as dealing with the licensing of these animals and the revocation of licenses.

<u>What is a 'guard dog'?</u>

Appears simple enough, but to clarify under the terms of the act. A guard dog is any dog which is being used to protect one or more of the following:

1. Premises (Property not including agricultural land or dwelling houses. So a person's house or flat would not be deemed premises under this Act. Neither would a farm. Any other form of property such as a business, factory, etc., would be deemed 'premises' under this Act).

2. Property kept on the premises (The dog is being used to protect items of property within the premises, rather than the premises itself).

3. A person guarding the premises or such property (So the Security Officer is protecting the premises and its property. The guard dog is used to protect the Security Officer)

Control of Guard Dogs

Section 1 of the Guard Dogs Act (1975) deals with the control of guard dogs. It states that a person cannot use (or permit the use of guard dogs at any premises unless the dogs 'handler' is on the premises and the dog is under the control of the handler at all times when it is being used.

Capable

The dog's handler must be 'capable' of controlling the dog. There is no legal definition of 'capable' within the scope of this Act, but this would run into the realms of common sense. So, if the handler is not strong enough to control the dog or the handler has two broken arms and a dislocated knee then we could safely assume that the handler is unable to control the dog and so the courts will too. Should something untoward happen, such as the dog breaks free from the handler and bites someone, if the handler could be considered 'not capable' of controlling the dog then the handler and/or the owner could be held liable for the actions of the dog as well as a breach of section 1(1) of the Guard dogs Act.

When the dog is not being used

The handler cannot be expected, realistically, to maintain physical control of the dog consistently. What if a toilet break is needed (for the handler, not the dog)?

The handler will have two options available to them here. Firstly is section 1(2)(a) which allows for the 'handler' to relinquish control of the guard dog to another 'capable' handler, thus passing on the responsibility and liability to that person.

The second option comes under Section 1(2)(b) of the Guard Dogs Act and states that when the dog is not being used it must be secured so it is not at liberty to move freely about the premises. This is very simple in that the dog must be securely tied to an immovable object or within a secure pound and that this must prevent it from going where it wants and with effect would still keep the dog 'under control'. Now if the dog breaks free from its leash, pound, etc, and bites someone, who is liable? Again the handler and/or the owner as the dog could not have been 'secure' if it escaped.

Warning signs

Section 1(3) makes it so that any area where a guard dog is used there must be clear signs warning of the presence of a guard dog and that these signs must be clearly displayed at each entrance to the premises.

Now the problem here is that there is no clear definition of 'entrance'. Would this just mean the doors and gates to the premises or property? What about the hole in the fence that a child could climb through? What about the fire escape? Would the fence surrounding the property be an entrance if someone were to climb it? The Guard Dogs Act does not make this clear but you can be assured that should a person climb through that unmarked hole in the fence and be confronted, or worse bitten, by a guard dog then they would have strong enough grounds to make a complaint or sue the handler and owner. The best option here is to be 110% certain. Ensure that every conceivable entrance to the premises is clearly signed and leave no room for error. Think clearly about not only the most obvious 'entrances', but also the least obvious 'routes of accesses.

Licenses

Sections 2 & 3 of the Guard Dogs Act (1975) make it illegal to keep a guard dog without a license. It is also an offence for a person to permit the use of a guard dog if they know, or have reasonable cause to believe, that the dog is not licensed.

Guard Dog licenses are issued on a 12 month basis by the local authority. They have a start date (usually the day they are issued and will run until 12 months later). The regulations and restrictions imposed upon these licenses are at the discretion of that authority. This means that should you wish to keep a guard dog, you must first apply to the local council department that is responsible for the control of these licenses. The local authority can retract a Guard Dog license at any time they see fit.

The license holder is only the person who 'keeps' the guard dog. It does not necessarily have to be the handler as many professional dog handlers use dogs which belong to another person such as the owner of the security company.

Under section 4 of the Act, should the local authority refuse to issue a Guard Dog license or remove the license before its prescribed time, or the applicant disagrees with the conditions of the license then they may appeal to the Magistrates' Court. The Court may then advise the local authority on any corrections or amendments if they also disagree.

THE COURT SECURITY OFFICER (DESIGNATION) REGULATION (2005)

The Court Security Officers (Designation) Regulation (2005) prescribes the conditions which must be satisfied before a person can be designated as a Court Security Officer. It also sets out the required training which must be fulfilled by all Court Security Officers as well as further requirements of identity.

Training for Court Security Officers

Sections 2(1) & 2(2) of the Court Security Officers Regulation (2005) set out the requirements of training before an Officer can be appointed to the role. Completing the training alone is not enough however. Documentary evidence must be available to prove that the training has been completed to a satisfactory standard. The training requirements are:

- Training in the duties and powers of a Court Security Officer, and
- Training in risk assessment, and
- Training in safe working practices, and
- Training in managing stress when dealing with threatening situations, and
- Training in techniques for restraining a person and removing them from a building, and

- Training in any other area that the Lord Chancellor may require (this does not have to be national training. Further training may be necessary dependent upon the Court and the building in which it sits, the Officer, or the area.

Not only are these requirements to be fulfilled before a person can be appointed as a Court Security Officer, but a requirement can be made that further training, or repeated training, must be taken at any point once the person is in the role.

Identity

Section 3 of the Court Security Officer Regulations (2005) requires a person, before they can be appointed, to provide:

Proof of their identity, and

To make a declaration as to whether they have any unspent criminal offences.

Section 3 also makes a requirement of the employing body to obtain a criminal record check of the person before any appointment is made.

POWERS OF ARREST

The Police and Criminal Evidence Act (1984) give the authority to any person, other than a Constable, to make an arrest, without warrant, for an indictable offence under Section 24(a). This means that any person may make an arrest for the following reasons:

- To prevent the offender causing physical injury to themselves or others, or
- To prevent the offender suffering physical injury, or
- To prevent loss of or damage to property, or
- To prevent a person making off before a constable can assume responsibility for them.

Nearly 25 years ago, before the introduction of The Police and Criminal Evidence Act (1984) (PACE), the powers of arrest by which a 'non-Constable' could use to detain a person were referred to as a "Citizens arrest". This was a common law power (not written legislation) and allowed a person to arrest on the spot for an offence, in order that the offender answers before the courts. Nowadays the term 'Citizens arrest" is still used to describe the arrest by anybody other than a Constable, however in principle it is a non-existent procedure and instead the law is much more defined on the rights to arrest by any person.

When can an arrest be made?

Arrests of offenders by any person, other than a Constable, can be made only for indictable and triable either-way offences. Not for summary offences. This means that arrests for only sufficiently serious offences such as theft (because it is triable either-way) can be made. The arrest can be made on:

1. Anyone who is in the act of committing an indictable offence (or you have reasonable grounds to suspect is committing and indictable offence), or

2. Anyone who has committed an offence (or you have reasonable grounds to suspect is committing and indictable offence).

The arrest can only be made if it is not reasonable for a Constable to do so at the time. This means that if there is a Constable stood nearby then you should get him or her to make the arrest. If not, it is your responsibility.

The difference between a Constables and a non-Constables arrest

As you can see, as a non-Constable you may arrest the offender either during the illegal act they are committing or immediately afterwards. A Constable derives his powers of arrest from Section 24 of PACE and this allows him to also arrest <u>before</u> the crime. A Constable may also arrest to:

1. enable the name or address of a person to be ascertained, or
2. to prevent an offence against public decency, or
3. to prevent an unlawful obstruction of the highway, or
4. to protect a child or vulnerable person, or
5. to allow a prompt and effective investigation of an offence, or
6. to prevent any prosecution for the offence from being hindered by the disappearance of the person being arrested

With or without warrant?

A warrant is an order, issued by the Courts to "arrest" a

person for a certain offence and the arrest warrant is issued to a Constable (the Office of a Constable is held by a number of civil servants including Police Officers, Prison Officers and some Border Agents). However, arrests without a warrant are also allowed by both Constables and yourselves.

THE CRIMINAL DAMAGE ACT (1971)

The Criminal Damage Act of (1971) sets out a number of general offences to protect property from harmful damage. Prior to this Act, damage to property was a common law offence and mainly concerned with damage to dwellings and supplies of food. As the years passed the need for a more refined set of offences led to the introduction of the Criminal Damage Act (1971). The Act covers damage caused by persons through wilful destruction or recklessness and, where fire is used, the Act establishes the charge of Arson.

The Criminal Damage Act also repealed other previous Acts of Parliament including the Dockyards, etc. Protection Act (1772) which allowed for the death penalty for the offence of "arson in Royal Dockyards".

DESTROYING OR DAMAGING PROPERTY

Section 1 of the Criminal Damage Act 1971 contains three parts (Sections 1(1), 1(2) & 1(3)). Section 1(1) is concerned with the general offence of unlawful damage whilst section 1(2) deals with that of 'Aggravated Criminal Damage'. Section 1(3) makes the offence to be charged as "Arson" where fire is used to destroy or damage property.

Section 1(1) Criminal Damage (or Simple Arson)

The first section of the Act creates the basic offence whereby a person who without lawful authority destroys or damages any property belonging to another with the intention to, or reckless as to, destroy or damage it.

Without lawful authority

Without lawful excuse is defined within Section 5 of the Criminal Damage Act 1971. It states that lawful excuse would include where the defendant believed that the person who should consent to the damage to property (usually the owner of the property in question) either had consented to it or would consent to it if they knew.

Lawful authority would also include where the damage was caused in order to protect other property and that the property was in immediate need of protection and the decision to damage was reasonable at the time. So, as an example, if you have two houses next to each other but separated by a garden shed. If the first house was on fire and a person pulled down and destroyed the garden shed between them in order to prevent the fire spreading to the second house then they would have a lawful excuse to do so. If at a later time, it was decided that there was really no need to have pulled down the shed after all as the fire service was only seconds away then that does not mean the defense is invalid. It only matters what the person at the time believed was the right thing to do at that particular moment.

Destroys or damages

There is of course a big difference between destroying and damaging. If property is destroyed it would imply that it is permanent. To damage would imply a temporary alteration in the state of the property. In fact any alteration to the physical nature of the property may amount to criminal damage. This is dependent upon the interference caused to the owner and the change to any value or usefulness of the property. If a person spits on a jacket which can be easily wiped clean then this would generally not be criminal damage as the item can be rectified and there is only really an inconvenience to the wearer. Likewise a scratch to a scaffolding pole (*Morphitis v. Salmon* (1990)) would not attract a charge of criminal damage as it would probably not affect is value or usefulness. On the other hand, a scratch to a car could affect its value and so would more likely attract a charge of criminal damage.

Property

Property which can be unlawfully damaged includes pretty much anything which is tangible (remember anything which you can touch and has a physical being), so this would include anything from a house to a boat to a child's toy. If the offender dumps waste onto land then he or she will have committed criminal damage to the land.

Belonging to another

The property must belong to another person to be an offence under section 1(1). A person cannot unlawfully damage their own property under this sub-section unless that property has a proprietary right or interest by a third party. So if a person destroys or damages their own house then they have not created an offence of criminal damage because it is their own property, but if that house has a mortgage on it, then the bank or mortgage provider has a proprietary interest in that property and so a charge of criminal damage can be established.

Remember though that 'belonging' (as with theft) does not necessarily mean the person that purchased the property. It means the person in possession and control at the time so I could loan you a pen which is then damaged by another person. The offence of criminal damage would be against property 'belonging' to you as it is you in possession and control of the pen.

Intention or recklessness

The offender must have either:

1. caused the damage intentionally (they meant to cause the damage), or

2. was reckless when they caused the damage (they were aware that there was a risk of damage in their actions yet they went onto take that risk). An appeal case held in the Divisional Court in 2006 (*Booth v. Crown Prosecution Service* (2006)) upheld the conviction of a person for criminal damage when they were found guilty of recklessly damaging a vehicle. The appellant rashly dashed into the road and in doing so he recklessly damaged the vehicle that hit him because "the appellant was aware of the risk and closed his mind to it".

3.

AGGRAVATED CRIMINAL DAMAGE (OR AGG. ARSON)

Section 1(2) of the Criminal Damage Act 1971 deals with the offence referred to as 'aggravated criminal damage'. As with criminal damage under section 1(1) the offender must destroy or damage property intending to do so or reckless as to doing so. The difference with this offence is that in doing so the offender intended to endanger the life of another or was reckless as to their actions endangering the life of another.

The property does not have to belong to another for aggravated criminal damage. A person can be guilty of this offence even if it is entirely their own property.

<u>Nobody's home</u>

As an example, an offender sets fire to a house which has nobody in it so there is no risk to life. The offender can still be guilty of aggravated criminal damage if he foresaw that there was a possibility that somebody could be home or he intended the damage to risk life. It does not matter that it turns out nobody was there.

ARSON

Section 1(3) of the Criminal Damage Act 1971 states that where the means used to cause criminal damage or aggravated criminal damage is by fire then the offence shall be charged as Arson (so 'Arson' for 'Criminal damage' and 'Aggravated Arson' for 'Aggravated criminal damage'). Where the charge is for arson the maximum sentence goes up to life imprisonment.

THREATS TO DESTROY OR DAMAGE PROPERTY

Section 2 of the Criminal Damage Act 1971 creates the offence of 'Threats to destroy or damage property'. If the offender makes a threat with the intention of putting a person in fear of another person's property being destroyed or damaged (section 1(1)) or putting another person in fear that any property will be damaged or destroyed in a way which is likely to endanger life (section 1(2)) then they will be guilty of this offence irrespective of whether they actually carry out the threat or intend upon carrying out the threat.

POSSESSING ANYTHING WITH INTENT TO DESTROY OR DAMAGE PROPERTY

Section 3 of the Criminal Damage Act 1971 creates an offence to have on your person, or under your control, any item which will either destroy or damage another person's property (section 1(1)) or any item which will destroy or damage property in a way which is likely to endanger life (section 1(2)). The item in question must be intended for that use. This means that if a person carries a box of matches then they are perfectly entitled to do so and will be committing no offence. If, however, they are carrying that same box of matches with the intention of setting fire to property with them then they will be committing an offence under section 3.

The idea behind this is that the offender can be apprehended and charged with an offence without necessarily waiting for them to actually commit the damage.

ASSAULTS

The law surrounding any form of assault by one person against another recognizes varying degrees of harm and intention. This means that (usually) a person who commits a greater degree of harm to another, or has the intention to seriously harm, will receive a greater penalty than the offender that only pushes a person over or recklessly injures someone. The more serious offences of assault are contained within the 'Offences Against the Person Act (1861)', whilst the less serious (Common Assault and Battery (both often referred to simply as 'Assaults')) are offences under the Criminal Justice Act (1988).

COMMON ASSAULT

<u>Summary Offence</u>

<u>Maximum sentence = 6 months imprisonment</u>

When the term "Common Assault" is used, it conjures up images of one person punching or kicking another with the end result being the victim suffering a minor injury such as a black eye. But is this correct? Common Assault is an offence under Section 39 of the Criminal Justice Act (1988).

The definition of 'Common Assault' does not come from legislation, but from case law. It states that a Common Assault is:

> *"any act which intentionally or recklessly, causes another person to apprehend immediate and unlawful personal violence"*

This definition comes from the Judge in the criminal appeal case '*Fagan* v. *Metropolitan Police Commissioner* [1969] 1 QB 439'. It means that for a Common Assault to take place there need be no actual 'touching' of the victim by the offender. It is only necessary that the victim thinks that he or she is about to be unlawfully touched.

So, for example, if the offender approaches the victim and says something along the lines of… "I am going to punch you in the head", and then raises his fists to signify this, then we can safely assume that the victim is under the impression they are about to get a punch. This is a Common Assault.

Words alone

The decisions of previous cases suggest that words alone can amount to a Common Assault. This means that, in the last example, if the offender only says "I am going to punch you in the head" but is at the time relaxes in an arm chair with a cup of coffee in his hand then this would still amount to a Common Assault even though there is no physical gesture (no raising of the fists) to signify an imminent assault.

The victim is not afraid

So the victim, in the previous example, turns out to be a heavyweight boxing champion. As such he is not intimidated or afraid of the guy threatening to punch him. Does this matter?

No, the victim only needs to be aware that there is a threat of violence or unlawful touching against him. It does not matter that he may not be frightened. So long as he thinks he is about to be unlawfully touched.

Immediate

The threat of force must be immediate. So an offender telling his victim that they will punch them in 2 and a half hours' time will not be committing a Common Assault (however, in 2 and a half hours' time, when they return, that will be when the Common Assault, or other assault, will take place).

Intention or recklessness

Again, the offender must have intended the victim to apprehend immediate and unlawful personal violence or had been reckless (knew there was a risk that the victim would fear unlawful touching, yet went onto to take that risk anyway). So, if a person is waving his fists in the air and shouting, (because his football team had just scored) but a passerby mistakenly believes this to be a violent threat towards them, there would be no offence. This is because the man waving his fists does not have the intention towards any victim and he could not have been reckless in his actions (how could he have known his actions would be seen in that way)?

BATTERY

Summary Offence

Maximum sentence = 6 months imprisonment

Where Common Assault is the apprehension of immediate and unlawful personal violence, Battery is the actual infliction of that violence.

So where we would have the Common Assault when the offender shook his fists and threatened the victim with a punch... We would have the battery when the offender actually punched the victim.

THE OFFENCES AGAINST THE PERSON ACT (1861)

The offences Against the Person Act (1861) is a very old Act of Parliament as you can see from the title year. Just how old can be seen from within, still valid, sections of the Act.

Section 17 of the OAPA (1861) creates the offence of "Impeding a person endeavoring to save himself from shipwreck" and this offence carries with it a maximum sentence of life imprisonment. Now, I would sincerely hope that this is not an offence you will ever come across, but it does demonstrate just how old this legislation is. There is, and has been a number of times before, plans by Parliament to introduce new legislation which will clearly set out a new range of offences replacing those of the OAPA (1861). They will be less archaic and written in a little more modern tone instead of the Victorian language used in this Act. New legislation will also, hopefully, more clearly summarize and define offences against the person by putting them into some sort of organized structure. This may take some time though.

The offences under the Offences Against the Person Act 1861, which you will deal with more often are 'Assault Occasioning Actual Bodily Harm (section 47), Wounding or inflicting Grievous Bodily Harm (section 20), and Wounding or inflicting Grievous Bodily Harm with Intent (section 17).

ASSAULT OCCASIONING ACTUAL BODILY HARM

Triable either-way

Maximum sentence = 5 years imprisonment

"any hurt or injury calculated to interfere with the health or comfort of the victim"

This definition of what amounts to Actual Bodily Harm (ABH) comes from the case of '*R* v. *Miller* [1954]'. It differs from Battery where Actual Bodily Harm is exactly as it says on the tin. "Actual harm".

Actual Bodily Harm is an offence under Section 47 of the Offences Against the Person Act (1861).

Amount of Actual Bodily Harm caused

The actual harm does not have to be serious. It could be a scratch or a bruise, so long as there is actual bodily harm and that harm interferes with the health or comfort of the victim. It must be harm caused as a direct result of the assault.

The cutting off of a substantial part of someone's hair can also amount to Actual Bodily Harm so the harm does not necessarily have to be something which creates physical pain.

Neither does it need to by physical. It can include psychiatric injury, although it must be a recognizable clinical condition which has been formed by the assault (such as neurosis or reactive depression). Anger or recurring fear will not suffice for this offence.

Intention or recklessness

Again, there must be intention or recklessness, but it only needs to be an intention or recklessness to commit the assault. It would be irrelevant whether the intention was to cause physical harm or whether the offender was reckless as to any harm being caused. Only that they intended, or were reckless, as to committing an assault.

WOUNDING OR INFLICTING GRIEVOUS BODILY HARM

<u>Triable either-way</u>

<u>Maximum sentence = 5 years imprisonment</u>

"Whosoever shall unlawfully and maliciously wound or inflict any grievous bodily harm upon any other person, either with or without any weapon or instrument"

Wounding or Inflicting Grievous Bodily Harm (often referred to as GBH) is an offence under Section 20 of the Offences Against the Person Act (1861). It is more serious than the previous offence of Assault Occasioning Actual Bodily Harm (s.47) but both offences carry the same maximum sentence of five years imprisonment and both offences are triable either-way. This, again, is due to the OAPA being outdated and in need of modernization. In practice, those offenders found guilty of Section 20 (GBH) will usually receive sentences closer to the maximum five years imprisonment as opposed to those found guilty of ABH whom will usually receive sentences towards the lower end of the scale.

<u>Maliciously</u>

Maliciously means "with intention or recklessness.

<u>Wounding</u>

So what is a wound? According to previous case law, a wound, for the purposes of Section 20, is anything which breaks both layers of the skin, i.e. causes it to bleed. It need not be a serious cut to be classed as a 'wound'. A small scratch will suffice so long as the skin is broken and blood is drawn.

Grievous Bodily Harm

Grievous Bodily Harm simply means "really serious harm".

With or without any weapon or other instrument

Exactly as it says… the wounding or GBH may be caused with or without a weapon. By 'instrument', the Act is referring to any other property which is used as a weapon. This could be an improvised cosh or anything else which would generally not be a weapon but has been used as such to commit this offence.

WOUNDING OR INFLICTING GRIEVOUS BODILY HARM WITH INTENT

Indictable offence

Maximum sentence = life imprisonment

"Whosoever shall unlawfully and maliciously by any means whatsoever wound or cause any grievous bodily harm to any person, . . . with intent, . . . to do some . . . grievous bodily harm to any person, or with intent to resist or prevent the lawful apprehension or

detainer of any person"

GBH with intent is an offence under Section 18 of the Offences Against the Person Act (1861). It is more serious and this is reflected in its higher maximum sentence of life imprisonment as well as being an indictable only offence (it can only be tried in the Crown Court before a Judge and jury).

Intention

The obvious difference between this offence and the previous Section 20 (GBH) is that there must be an intention to cause the victim "really serious harm" or the offence must have been committed in order to prevent or resist a lawful arrest and, in the course of doing so, an intention, or recklessness, that some harm might occur.

Where the offender intended to cause GBH, they must only have had the intention to cause Grievous Bodily Harm, and not been reckless as to the Grievous Bodily Harm (as how could they have recklessly intended to cause the harm)??

Where the offender causes harm in order to prevent or resist a lawful arrest, they must either have intended to cause really serious harm in the process or, this time, they could have been reckless as to the really serious harm being caused. For example, a Police Officer is making an arrest when, in order to evade arrest, the offender pushes the Police Officer over causing them really serious harm. They may not have intended the really serious harm but they did intend to evade arrest and would have known that by pushing the Officer over there was a risk of harm, yet they went on to take that risk. This would make them guilty of Section 18, GBH with intent. There is no previous case law with regards this offence when a Security Officer is making an arrest. However, it would more than likely still apply as it is still a lawful arrest where the Security Officer is making it.

UNINTENTIONAL CONTACT

Something which happens far too often is when a Security Officer, whilst making an arrest touches the offender in order to guide them. For example a Store Detective may touch the arm of the offender and point to where he or she expects them to go. There is no harm intended and no harm caused. It is a simple gesture. This is perfectly acceptable. But many offenders will use the "don't touch me, that's an assault" reaction. It is not an assault. It is perfectly recognized by the courts that everyday forms of contact will happen between people. If you place your hands on a person's arm or shoulder to signify that you are speaking directly to them or to guide them, then you are as entitled to do that as you would be to tap your friends on the shoulder and let them know you are there. In fact, it used to be common practice to touch the offenders arm when informing the offender you were arresting them (this is because some offenders used to claim they did not realize it was them being arrested, they thought you were speaking to somebody else). So if you ever come across the "you touched me, that's an assault" claim, understand that you are perfectly within your rights and the offender is just trying their luck.

THE USE OF FORCE

The Use of Force is permitted under Section 3(1) of the 1967 Criminal Law Act and Section 76 of the Criminal Justice and Immigration Act 2008

Section 3(1) of The Criminal Law Act 1967 states:

"a person may use such force as is reasonable in the circumstances in the prevention of crime, or in effecting or assisting in the lawful arrest of offenders or suspected offenders or of persons unlawfully at large"

<u>Such force as is reasonable</u>

So we can see that the use of reasonable force may be used for:

1. The prevention of crime, or
2. in self-defense.

But what is, and how much force, would be 'reasonable'? If I attempted to slap you with the back of my hand, would it be reasonable for you to defend yourself by hitting me back with a baseball bat and then jumping on my head? Perhaps it would? More likely not though.

How much force is reasonable in the circumstances is for the person using the reasonable force to decide and this ultimately would be tested by the Judge and jury. So if you used 'reasonable force', the degree to which that force was used would be determined according to the circumstances that you found yourself in. If you honestly believed that the only way to defend yourself from my slap was to hit me with a baseball bat and then jump on my head then that would be self-defense. Nobody else could have made that decision for you and so it is for you to judge what is reasonable.

The same reasoning would apply if that belief was a mistaken one. So if Mr. A believes that Mr. B is about to attack him and Mr. A reacts by striking Mr. B first (in self-defense), then it emerges that Mr. A was in fact mistaken and Mr. B had no intention of assaulting him whatsoever, then will the defense of self-defense still be plausible?

Yes it would. The test of reasonableness is judged upon what Mr. A honestly believed it to be at the time. If matters not that Mr. A was mistaken (in the eyes of the law anyway) only that he believed he was about to be attacked and that he took, what he regarded as, reasonable steps to prevent that.

Section 76 of The Criminal Justice and Immigration Act 2008 states:

> *"where a person seeks to rely on a defense of self-defense or acting in prevention of a crime, the issue of whether the force used by the defendant was reasonable is to be determined according to the circumstances as the defendant believed them to be*

This test is, however, two-fold. That is because anybody could claim that they honestly believed that hitting back with baseball bats and jumping on heads would be a valid defense to a charge of assault and so there must be some form of regulation there or it would be chaos. So, if it were believed that your use of force was over exercised or was not equivalent to the degree of threat, or perhaps it was believed that you could have run away and called the Police rather than use force, then this can be tested by the courts. If the Judge or jury decide that the force used by you was excessive then your claim of 'self-defense' will have failed and you will be liable for the assault.

Prevention of crime

The use of force is allowed in the prevention of <u>any</u> crime. Not just assaults. So force may be reasonably used in the prevention of a burglary, rape, murder, etc., etc…

In the end the use of force, whether in self-defense or to prevent crime/make a lawful arrest, should never be taken lightly. It is for your own common sense to dictate what actions should be taken. It can be so easy to overstep that boundary and end up on the wrong side of the law. You will not go wrong by always thinking to yourself:

1. "am I using the minimum amount of force I can", and
2. "what other options are there"?

Follow those simple rules and you will not go wrong.

THE CRIMINAL ATTEMPTS ACT 1981

Indictable offence

Maximum sentence = dependent on the offence

Believe it or not, Criminals do not always succeed in the crimes they are attempting to commit. But does this mean that if they are unsuccessful they are not liable for any offence?

Section 1(1) of the Criminal Attempts Act 1981 states:

"If, with intent to commit an offence to which this section applies, a person does an act which is more than merely preparatory to the commission of the offence, he is guilty of attempting to commit the offence"

This means that to be liable for an attempted offense the offender needs to have:

1. the intention to commit the offense, and
2. must have done something more than merely preparatory towards the commission of the offense.

The type of offense which can be 'attempted'

Only indictable offences can be attempted (those tried

in the Crown Court). Not summary offences. So a person cannot be guilty of attempting to commit a Common Assault because that is a summary offence (triable only in the Magistrates' Court).

More than merely preparatory

So at what stage of the attempt would this be?

There are no strict guidelines telling us at what stage of a crime we would have gone past the point of preparing to commit the offense. Eventually it would be for the Judge to decide whether the act was more than merely preparatory. For us though it would require common sense.

If an offender plans on committing an armed robbery then there will be stages they may go through before the offense is completed. Perhaps they will start first by buying a map of the local streets to plan their 'getaway'.

Perhaps next they will take photographs of the bank?? These would be preparatory.

The offender may go and buy the gun he needs for the robbery… Again this would still be preparatory.

On the day of the robbery he could sit in wait outside the bank, waiting for the right opportunity… Now we are heading towards the realms of more than merely preparatory. But even waiting ready outside may be argued as still preparatory.

Finally the robber bursts through the doors to the bank and shouts "This is a robbery"!! Now this would certainly be passed the point of merely preparatory and so the attempted offense has now been committed.

This is the reason why Police will sit in wait (during a Stakeout) if they are aware an offense is going to be committed. A few years back there was a rather large attempted robbery at the Millennium Dome. The robbers planned on stealing the 'Millennium Diamond'. You may remember this?

Now the Police knew of the planning of this offense months in advance. If it were not for the requirement of waiting until the act was more than merely preparatory they could have arrested the gang long before and saved lots of money and effort. But instead Police lay in wait, disguised as cleaners and sightseers and just waiting for the gang to come charging in. Eventually the gang arrived (in a JCB, which they kindly drove through the front doors). At this point the crime was more than merely preparatory as the gang were now in the process of committing the robbery. At that point Police could move in and arrest.

Arresting for the attempted offense

There may be occasions where it would be unsafe or uncertain to make an arrest for a crime after the offense has been committed and so an arrest for the attempted offense may be required. This could happen during a shop theft where there may be a risk of arresting outside of the store because the 'shoplifter' has a group of friends waiting. Or if the main offense is Criminal Damage or Arson it may be unwise to let the offender commit the crime before we stop them (for obvious reasons). This is where an arrest or complaint can be made for the attempted offense.

The crime was impossible

Assume now that we have a pickpocket on site… The pickpocket puts his hand into a strangers coat pocket, hoping to find a wallet I presume. Instead the pocket is empty and the pickpocket gets nothing. Has an offense still been committed? After all if there is no wallet or car keys in the pocket how could there be an offense as it would have been impossible to steal them if they were not there?

Yes the pickpocket is still guilty of attempted theft. This is because Section 1(2) & 1(3) of The Criminal Attempts Act 1981 state that where the offender believes it to be so, he would have had an intention to commit the offense and that would be sufficient. In other words, the impossibility to commit the offense is no defense. If the offender has the intention to commit the offense then they are still guilty of it.

Sentences

A person found guilty of an attempted offence faces the same penalties as if the offence itself had been completed. So a person found guilty of attempted theft faces maximum imprisonment of up to seven years, the same as if they were found guilty of having committed a theft.

HUMAN RIGHTS IN BRIEF

THE EUROPEAN CONVENTION ON HUMAN RIGHTS

The European Convention on Human Rights came into force in 1953 as a result of the Second World War. It is quite often mistakenly regarded as a part of the European Union. It is not. The European Union and the European Convention on Human Rights (ECHR) are two completely different entities.

The ECHR sets out various civil, political, economic, social, and cultural rights and freedoms which are to be guaranteed to the people of each State (country) signed up to the Convention.

The rights protected under the ECHR are:

(art.2) The Right to Life

(art.3) Freedom from torture or inhumane or degrading treatment or punishment)

(art.4) Freedom from slavery or compulsory Labour

(art.5) The right to civil liberty and security of the person

(art.6) The right to a fair trial by an impartial tribunal

(art.7) The prohibition of retrospective criminal laws

(art.8) The right to respect for people's privacy, including their homes and correspondence

(art.9) The right to freedom of thought, conscience

and religion

(art.10) Freedom of expression

(art.11) Freedom of peaceful assembly and association, including the right to join trade unions

(art.12) The right marry and found a family

As well as these Articles there are a number of further rights protected by 'Protocols' under the ECHR. These include the abolition of the death penalty and the right to education and peaceful enjoyment of possessions.

In the United Kingdom, Parliament is supreme. This means that nobody can tell Parliament what it can and cannot do. Parliament may make any law it so wishes and no other entity may make laws without the express permission of Parliament. This is why we have The Human Rights Act 1998.

The Human Rights Act 1998 does not guarantee us any rights. It simply ensures that rights under the ECHR are applicable to English law. In effect, the Human Rights Act 1998 is the 'transport' which makes the European Convention a part of UK law. The Human Rights Act 1998 also forces UK Courts to 'hear' breaches of the ECHR and find remedies for them rather than every person having to apply directly to the European Court of Human Rights in Strasbourg.

Now how does this apply to private Security? Well often offenders will claim that there is a breach of their Human Rights when they are being detained. These offenders do not know what they are talking about. The European Courts, and UK Courts where they hear breaches of Human Rights, do hear cases between private citizens (known as 'Horizontal effect') but mainly any breaches are committed by the Government or a department of Government against a citizen ('Vertical effect'). It is almost impossible for a private citizen to breach a human right without breaking an already in place UK law.

Should I, as a private citizen, wish to withdraw another person's right to life, I will not be in breach of Article 2 (The Right to Life). I will be in breach of the common law of Murder. Likewise if I tortured another human being I would not be in breach of Article 3 but, instead, will have committed an Assault offence. So provided you have not committed an offence prohibited by law then you will not have acted in breach of a person's human rights.

THE PRIVATE SECURITY INDUSTRY ACT 2001

The Private Security Industry Act 2001 was introduced to regulate and improve the private security industry. It attempts to do this by setting minimum standards for private Security Officers and introducing the Security Industry Authority (SIA) to ensure these standards and regulated and maintained.

THE SECURITY INDUSTRY AUTHORITY (SIA)

Prior to the establishment of the Security Industry Authority, the Security Industry suffered from a fast turnaround of staff and poor standards of training. This was mainly due to increased competition between Security companies and so the lower each company tendered their contract, the more likely they would win that contract. This again resulted in lower wages and longer hours. The next Security Company would then tender an even lower contract and the next set of Security Officers were paid even less and received even less training. It became a downwards spiral. Employment within the security industry was underpaid and undervalued and the services offered were of an extremely poor standard. Businesses forced through necessity to contract Security Officers, done so begrudgingly as it became a cost they did not want.

The objective of the Security Industry Authority was to ensure, through regulation, that Officers were vetted and checked thoroughly before being allowed into a position of trust. It also aimed to ensure a minimum standard of training for industry staff. This in turn would improve the standards of service within the industry and that in turn would improve wages whilst maintaining public safety.

Now standards within Private Security have improved immensely. The role of a Security Officer is now seen as a career choice rather than "a job to make do with". Security Officers are able to deal with far more complex tasks and the respect given by agencies such as the Police has much improved.

LICENSING

Section 3 of the PSIA 2001 makes it an offence to perform a role, which requires licensing, without the relevant license. Any person found guilty of this faces, on Summary conviction, up to six months imprisonment and/or a £5,000 fine.

Licensable activities include:

- Security Guarding
- Key Holding
- Cash and Valuables in Transit
- Close Protection
- Door Supervision

- Public Space Surveillance (CCTV)

VEHICLE IMMOBILISATION

The SIA had previously also licensed all forms of vehicle immobilisation services. This, however, changed with the introduction of Chapter 2 of The Protection of Freedoms Act 2012. This Act created an offence of 'vehicle immobilisation' without lawful authority. It is now an offence to attach an 'immobilising device' (such as a wheel clamp) or restrict the movement of any vehicle intending to prevent or inhibit the moving of the vehicle. The only exception to this would be where a vehicle has been parked on private land and that land has a fixed barrier in place (and the barrier was in place when the vehicle arrived). The barrier may be used to restrict the movement of the vehicle (for example the barrier in a car park would prevent the vehicle from leaving without first making payment).

SIA LICENCES

There are currently two types of SIA license available:

- A 'Front line' license. This is the popular 'identity card' style license which must be worn for all licensable activities.

- A 'Non-front line' license. This is a letter issued by the SIA to those that manage, supervise and employ front line staff.

IN-HOUSE GUARDING

Many businesses, such as department stores, will hire their own 'in-house' security rather than external contract guards. In house security is not regulated by the SIA and no form of licensing is required.

Originally, the intention of Parliament and the SIA was to eventually regulate in-house security but this idea has since been dropped. It was decided that there was no real need to license in-house as it proved unnecessary and would make no significant improvement to public protection.

ACS – APPROVED CONTRACTOR SCHEME

Further to individual licensing, the SIA also manage an Approved Contractor Scheme (ACS). This scheme is entirely voluntary and means that Security businesses can opt into a quality assurance scheme. This scheme assesses the company against a number of operational and performance standards. If the company is successfully marked in this scheme they are awarded an 'Approved Contractor' status. This status is re-registered each year by the Security Company and every third year they are reassessed to keep the award.

DATA PROTECTION ACT 1998

The Data Protection Act 1998 was created by Parliament in order that the UK comply with The European Data Protection Directive of 1995. It also replaced two former pieces of legislation (The Data Protection Act 1984 and The Access to Personal Files 1987). The European Data Protection Directive 1995 required its Member States to protect its citizens right to privacy with regards the processing of personal information.

The Data Protection Act 1998 does this by legally obliging anyone that holds personal data (on either computers or 'relevant filing systems) to comply with the Act through eight 'data protection principles'. It does not apply to things 'personal'. So a CCTV camera installed in your home as security will not need to comply with the Act. Neither will a personal address book with your friends and families details in. Anything more than personal does need to comply with the principles of the Act.

RIGHTS AFFORDED TO THE CITIZEN

As a citizen of the United Kingdom, you, or anybody else, have:

- The right to view data an organisation holds

on them (a small fee may be charged for this)

- Request that incorrect information be corrected. If the company ignores your request then a court can order the data to be corrected or destroyed, and in some cases compensation can be awarded.
- Require that data is not used in any way that may potentially cause damage or distress.
- Require that their data is not used for direct marketing.

DATA PROTECTION PRINCIPLES AND THERE RELATION TO CCTV

The use of Closed Circuit Television (CCTV) in the United Kingdom is fast increasing. The UK now uses more CCTV per citizen than anywhere else in Europe. Security Officers using CCTV will have to daily comply with data protection principles where they apply to CCTV.

1. Principle 1 of the Data Protection Act 1998 covers the initial assessment of the CCTV system including the reasoning behind the use of CCTV should be established. Is it appropriate for the type of business? Also who is the person or organisation responsible for the system and its compliance?

2.   Principle 2 covers the location of the cameras. The equipment should be used to monitor only its intended spaces and where the cameras border other property they should be positioned so as not to overlook the other property as much as is practicable. The owners and residents of the 'bordered' property should also be consulted. Signs must also be displayed which are clearly visible to the public, on entering the premises being monitored, and must include information on who is the person or organisation responsible for the cameras and how to contact them and the purpose of the scheme (such as to deter shoplifters or monitor public safety). Principle 2 also ensures that the operators of the CCTV are aware of its purpose and that the CCTV can only be used for such purposes.

Where the CCTV is used for covert purposes, and advertising their whereabouts and purpose is impractical, the cameras must be for a specific criminal activity. This means that covert cameras cannot be hidden in a stock room, for example, in the hope of catching a thief. There must be a specific crime being monitored, so if there have been previous thefts from the same stock room and the cameras are for the purposes of monitoring that particular series of thefts then that would be acceptable. The operator of the covert cameras must document the specific criminal activity being monitored and that there is a need to use surveillance to obtain the evidence required and that the use of signs would prejudice the success of obtaining such evidence.

3. Data Protection Principles 1, 6, & 7 cover Access by Data Subjects (persons being monitored by the CCTV, or in field of view of the CCTV). This means that people entering a premises being monitored by CCTV have a right to apply for access to their information (images for the purpose of CCTV). The premises using CCTV should have some type of request form which should provide space for the applicant to write the information required to locate the specific images and how they can be identified (such as in a certain area at a certain time wearing a blue raincoat). The form should also indicate where there is a fee to be paid and how much and ask whether merely viewing the images would satisfy the individual. A designated person within the organisation must then make a decision whether any third parties must be informed (such as other persons in the same images) and they must be responsible for the locating of those images and deal with the showing of the images to the applicant.

The designated person may refuse permission, in writing, for the applicant to view their images where there is good reason and must provide a clear complaints procedure. Where this permission is refused it must be documented when the date of the request was made and who made the request as well as the reason for refusing to supply the images. This must be signed and named by the person making the decision not to provide the images. Refusal or acceptance of the application to view the images must be made within 40 days of receiving the required fee.

The applicant (or data subject) may take court action to prevent unlawful processing of the information and can claim compensation for 'damages' suffered as a result of any breaches of the Data Protection Act 1998.

4.   Principles 3, 5, & 7 ensure that images must not be retained for longer than is necessary. Where images are kept for evidential purposes they must be kept in a secure place with controlled access and stored away from other routine data.

These principles also ensures that access to images is restricted to only designated staff and that the viewing of any images must be in a restricted area.

5. Principles 3, 4, & 5 ensure the quality of the data. This means that equipment should   be checked to ensure it performs correctly and maintained and serviced. They should   also be protected from vandalism and have clear procedures for making repairs.

If VHS tapes are used they must be of good quality and the maximum number of passes must be no more than 13 times. The tapes should be wiped after each use to prevent recording one image over another.

TRESSPASS

A person trespasses if they illegally enter land or premises. All land is owned by somebody so in effect a person trespasses if they enter any land without permission (unless it is a public right of way or public path).

Under English law, trespassing is usually not a criminal offence, so signs displaying "Trespassers will be prosecuted" do not have real effect and are there as a scare tactic only. Only in some circumstances will there be a criminal wrong for trespassing. These situations are covered by Part V of the Criminal Justice and Public Order Act 1994 and include specific offences for trespassing (for example for raves, hunt saboteurs, mass trespass, and trespass by squatters). These criminal offences can only be upheld by a Constable. There are also criminal offences for trespassing in certain important places such as residences in Downing Street and certain Government buildings and Royal residences.

Most actions against trespass are a civil wrong and as such are dealt with through the civil courts. A person can be sued if they trespass (for the hypothetical value of the benefit gained in trespassing). The landowner can also ask for an injunction to be issued to the trespasser preventing them from trespassing on that land in future. If the trespasser trespasses after receiving this injunction then they will still not be committing a criminal offence in trespassing but will be committing the criminal offence of 'Contempt of Court' for which they can be fined or imprisoned.

NEIGHBOURS BOUNDARIES

The neighbour of private premises may have access to the private land for the purposes of repairing their own property (only basic preservation works) under the Neighbouring Land Act 1992 and written notification must be given to the landowner before any repairs begin.

DETERRING TRESPASSERS

A landowner is within his rights to construct 'obstacles' to prevent trespassing (such as walls or fences with metal spikes) although the local authorities have the power to remove obstacles where they pose a danger and are close to a public right of way. Some forms of obstacles would also be illegal. Some forms of barbed wire have now been banned. Also 'extreme' deterrents could also put the landowner in serious trouble. If the landowner lays traps which will harm a person they could receive criminal charges for the harm caused to the trespasser or even for the attempted offence if no trespasser has yet come across them. It would be down to common sense where obstacles are used to prevent trespass.

TABLE OF CASES

R v. Pittwood (1902) 19 TLR 37

House of Lords case R v. *T* [2009] LAC 310

R v Ghosh [1982] EWCA Crim 2

Morphitis v. Salmon (1990

Booth v. Crown Prosecution Service (2006)

Fagan v. *Metropolitan Police Commissioner* [1969] 1 QB 439

R v. *Miller* [1954] 2 QB 282)

R v. *Chan-Fook* [1994] 1 WLR 689

Moriarty v. *Brookes* (1834) 6 C & P 684

DPP v. *Smith* [2006] EWHC 94, [2006] 1 WLR 1571

TABLE OF LEGISLATION

Accessories and Abettors Act 1861

Crime and Disorder Act 1998

Theft Act 1968

Theft Act 1978Dockyards, etc. Protection Act (1772)

Criminal Justice Act 1988

Offences Against the Person Act 1861

Fraud Act 2006

Criminal Damage Act 1971

Criminal Law Act 1967ECHR

Human Rights Act 1998

Criminal Attempts Act 1981

Private security industry act 2001

Protection of Freedoms Act. 2012

The European Data Protection Directive of 1995
The Data Protection Act 1984
The Access to Personal Files Act 1987
Criminal Justice and Public Order Act 1994
Neighboring Land Act 1992

www.ingramcontent.com/pod-product-compliance
Lightning Source LLC
Chambersburg PA
CBHW051707170526
45167CB00002B/575